Learning What Love Means

SEMIOTEXT(E) NATIVE AGENTS SERIES

Originally published as *Ce qu'aimer veut dire*. © P.O.L éditeur, 2011.
This translation © 2017 by Semiotext(e).

Published by Semiotext(e)
PO BOX 629, South Pasadena, CA 91031
www.semiotexte.com

Cover: Hervé Guibert, "Michel Foucault, 1981."
Design: Hedi El Kholti

ISBN: 978-1-58435-186-3
Distributed by The MIT Press, Cambridge, Mass. and London, England
Printed in the United States of America

Mathieu Lindon

Learning What Love Means

Translated by Bruce Benderson

Contents

Love on the Run

I am perfectly aware that calling this book a *spiritual auto-biography* is placing it into a curious perspective. After all, it is a product of the tradition of French literature and its dependence upon certain cultural tenets of Catholicism. The spiritual autobiography, on the other hand, is firmly rooted in the English Protestant tradition of the seventeenth century. The most well known examples are John Bunyan's *Grace Abounding* (1666) and his allegory *The Pilgrim's Progress from This World, to That Which Is to Come* (1678). Such texts were originally real-life testaments of conversion by religious dissenters, with linear plots taking the reader from a state of damnation to an epiphany leading to the state of grace.

As creative nonfiction, Mathieu Lindon's *What Love Means* is neither a linear narrative nor a religious story. The book is a collage of free-associated episodes and interpretations that together compose for the reader a kind of manual about how to love; or, at least, this is what the book became for me. Nevertheless, as he runs from apartment to apartment, job to job, or lover to lover, the book becomes a story of conversion testifying to an author's radical change of viewpoint, which leads to his invitation into the social world through lessons about love.

Fundamentally, but not entirely, Lindon's *What Love Means* is a dialectic between two kinds of love—of a father and of a friend—from the standpoint of a gay man. These kinds of love interweave in rather surprising ways. Two men, often at opposite poles but also supplementing each other's influence, form the crux of the book: Jérôme Lindon, the author's father, who was also the lifetime friend of Samuel Beckett, as well as the discoverer and influential publisher of les Éditions de Minuit, which almost singlehandedly dominated mid-century literature by fostering the revolution of the *nouveau roman*; and Michel Foucault, whose ground-breaking sociological and philosophical texts challenged assumptions about the self, psychology, sex, pathology, and punishment with ideas that currently flourish in the curricula of most of our institutions of higher learning. Even so, if you're expecting an extended discussion of Foucaultian philosophy in this book, be aware that you will not find it. Instead, *What Love Means* is a personal redemptive work on a deep level, and probably one of the few contemporary texts as effective as the original seventeenth century spiritual autobiographies in taking the reader through passages creating a fundamental change in self-awareness.

Another factor that makes this book a highly original work is its nearly complete disregard for what has come to be called—especially in this country—identity politics. Redemption in this text does involve a gay author's harnessing of his own genital power and his ability to love, but this new power comes not so much from confrontation with and liberation from society's prejudices, as most "coming out" books are wont to do, but from his increasingly mature experiences of love, friendship and sex, with Michel Foucault acting (without trying to) as mentor and liberator to counteract the many negative and seemingly unsolvable problems brought on by the intense paternal bond the author shares with his father. In this sense, *What Love Means* is a coming-of-age novel tracing the author's life from a "hellish adolescence" to full personhood and membership in society. What also emerges in fragments is a portrait of Michel Foucault, the friend whose placid acceptance of the qualities and choices the author has experienced as torturous, whose knack for seeing conflict as instructive rather than character defaming, and whose ability to recast sexual desire in a new light transforms the author's world view.

Most literary historians believe that the fictionalization of the spiritual autobiography led to the birth of the Western novel in the eighteenth century, with such well-known examples as Defoe's *Robinson Crusoe*, a book that resembles *What Love Means* in a few fundamental ways. In Defoe's novel, the protagonist is punished for going against the will of his father and opting for a life of adventure. In *What Love Means*, Lindon's journey partly begins with his father's attempt when he publishes his first book to force him to use a pseudonym that won't shame the family. In addition, the prodigal Crusoe arrives at his island in total despair but learns faith through reading the Bible to gradually build a new world completely in his vision. Lindon also leaves the family nest and encounters friends and professional experiences that allow him to recast his world in more dynamic and less shame-inspiring colors. Not only Foucault but also other talented writers, such as Hervé Guibert and Alain Robbe-Grillet (both published by his father's house), jumpstart his achievements as a writer and sanction his erotic impulses.

Loosely considered, the spiritual autobiography still flourishes today (*ad nauseam*, I might add) in the often banal and clichéd redemptive narrative, characterizing a large percentage of novels and films dealing with addiction, crime, mental illness, and practically any life experience to which can be appended a "happy ending." The addict finds recovery, the criminals pay their debt to society, and the mentally ill find the cure that reinstates them in the world. *What Love Means* is no such animal. For one thing, drugs—heroin, opium and especially LSD—abound in this memoir, never once becoming a defect in character from which the protagonist must be saved. In fact, acid becomes one of the "elixirs" whose effects not only cement the growing friendship between the author and his talented friends, including Michel Foucault, but also the stimulus to insights about himself and his relationships. Like the more conventional memoirs that deal with drug use, this memoir is also about shame, but not the shame of drug use, which the author does not feel. It is about the shame inspired by the author's dissatisfactions concerning his identity, his passivity, and the parts of his character he feels are being rejected by his father, including his homosexuality.

Mathieu Lindon's "hellish adolescence" was an extremely solitary one. It occurred almost perpetually shut up in his room, where, as his friend Alain Robbe-Grillet jokes, he "spent [his] entire life reading." Family life for him was certainly far different than it is for most. Not only was his father descended from an illustrious Jewish French family that could boast a judge and former mayor; shortly after World War II he had taken the reins of les Éditions de Minuit, which had operated clandestinely in the shadow of the Occupation. From it he built a postwar publishing empire that could boast two Nobel Prize winners (Samuel Beckett and Claude Simon) and a vast array of other globally respected avant-gardists, including novelists Robbe-Grillet, Marguerite Duras and Robert Pinget. The charge Jérôme Lindon received from life came from his overwhelming literary power. It was an aesthetic power he exercised in the most stringent and judicious way, even placing financial profit beneath the pleasure of fostering and controlling talent. Mathieu Lindon spent his childhood and adolescence surrounded at the dinner table by his father's luminaries, embarrassedly conscious of his role as an appendage, a presence sanctioned only by family connections and not by any achievement. His goal was to change his status and become a writer in his own right. This identity had not yet been attained when, barely out of adolescence, he met Michel Foucault, who cheerfully turned over his luxury Parisian apartment to Mathieu and other friends his age every time Foucault left to travel, sometimes for extended periods. The Foucault apartment in this book takes on a strong identity of its own as an unfettered terrain for experiments with drugs and sexual adventures. In it the author finally builds an identity that is increasingly detached from the strictures of family life. Then, over the many dinners at the apartment that Lindon enjoys with Foucault whenever he's in town, Lindon discovers his perfect confidante with whom he can share all his thoughts and all his problems. Despite such mentorship, Lindon is careful to distinguish his bond with Foucault from a paternal bond. Foucault is easily old enough to be his father—a little more than a year younger than Lindon's father, in fact—but unlike his father, has no need for power over any aspect of their relationship. Deeply attached to his father as Lindon is, he portrays him as a "colonizer," who treats his son and his writers with the same emphasis on control. He is burdened all his life by what a quarreling colleague characterizes using the sentence, "Of course, you're always right." Conversely, none of Foucault's friends or associates are "colonial subjects." Like the gardener he is (he's fond of the large banana plant he nurtures on his balcony), his greatest joy is watching and helping his friends to bloom in their own way, no matter how eccentric, never judging or directly "educating" them. As a result, he enjoys several unconventional friendships, and this approach to the social world will eventually rub off on Mathieu Lindon.

Foucault died from HIV in 1984 after six wonderful years of intimate friendship with the author. The author's close friend Hervé Guibert succumbed to the same disease in 1991. Lindon's father passed away in 2001, after conflicts between father and son had been worked out and the son was finally able to benefit from his rich legacy. One of the most striking aspects of this coming-of-age spiritual autobiography is the relationship Lindon establishes between love and death. The most traumatic event in his life was Foucault's shockingly sudden disappearance, which left Lindon so bereft he never thought he would recover from it. If that were the case, this book would probably not exist. However, he would gradually discover that love transcends physical disappearance, and not just in the static sense. The love you receive from a friend, lover or father is the seed embedded in your intellect and emotions that keeps growing and slowly becomes your own transformation. In this book, Lindon quite unnecessarily admits, "I'm a necrophile: I keep loving the dead." Both he and the reader, however, quickly dispense with such a sinister observation. Just a few sentences after it, he acknowledges something he has already made obvious: "This book," he writes, "has been my way of taking my own loves captive."

— Bruce Benderson, New York City, 2017

Learning What Love Means

TEARS IN MY EYES

While looking for a book, my eyes fall upon another—what reader or author hasn't had the same experience?

I'm looking for a grammar book to check a rule of agreement and instead find a collection of writings in English by Willa Cather that I bought ages ago in a New York bookstore and never opened. I love that American writer's stories—their sweetness and generosity make my eyes swell as they recount all the solemn brutality of life's confrontations. But this collection, intended for those over the age of forty, isn't fiction. There's an essay on Thomas Mann's *Joseph and his Brothers*, another on Katherine Mansfield; all of it of interest to me, despite the fact that I hadn't looked at it since I bought it.

The title of the first essay is "A Chance Meeting," which I would have translated into French as "Une rencontre de fortune" after I'd read the piece, because the first sentence snags my attention, even though there's nothing extraordinary about it ("It happened at Aix-les-Bains, one of the pleasantest places in the world."); and I begin to absorb every single word. Willa Cather, who was fifty-three that August 1930, had come down to the Grand Hotel with someone she knew well—English leaving the gender unspecified—but of the same sex, I surmise, that often being the case when such an imprecision remains; and a biography confirms this for me. In fact, it was Edith Lewis, a close friend of the writer. Staying at the same hotel is an elderly French woman, at least 80, who takes all her meals alone and goes up to her room after dinner unless she comes out again for a driver to take her to an opera.

One evening without opera, she's smoking in the hotel drawing room and speaks to Willa Cather, advising she keep her answer simple, due to the other woman's lack of practice in English, no longer mastering it as well as she had in the past. This old lady, who lives in Antibes but is wild about the music you can hear in Aix, mentions Wagner and César Franck. A few days later, the writer and her friend encounter the eighty-year-old again. After a reference to the Russian Revolution, Edith Lewis expresses the opinion that such great Russian writers as Gogol, Tolstoy, Turgenev were lucky not to have lived long enough to experience it. "Ah yes," says the old lady, "for Turgenev, especially, all this would have been very terrible. I knew him well at one time."

Willa Cather writes of being astonished, then reflecting that it is possible the woman is so old that she would have been able to know Turgenev, even if this is Cather's first encounter with someone like that. The old lady smiles and answers that she often saw him as a young girl, and that because Turgenev was a close friend of her uncle, he'd correct her translation of *Faust*; and Willa Cather notices the woman's growing excitement as she speaks of him, her voice warming and her eyes brightening. The old lady goes on, "My mother died at my birth, and I was brought up in my uncle's house. He was more than a father to me. My uncle also was a man of letters, Gustave Flaubert, you may perhaps know..." Willa Cather indicates that these last words are said in a curious tone, as if the old lady had mentioned something indiscreet; and the meaning of this only comes to her slowly, the discovery that the octogenarian in front of her is the

"Caro" of *Lettres à sa nièce Caroline*, a book that Cather has of course read since she's such a great admirer of Flaubert. And she is moved, suddenly coming upon a mountain of memories, as if the great moments of nineteenth century French literature had suddenly become so close she could almost reach out to take hold of them.

In Willa Cather, I love the benevolence and spontaneous nobility with which her characters think and act. She's the only author I know, except for the Austrian Adalbert Stifter in the nineteenth century, whose heroes always evolve to the highest level without their losing plausibility. In my reading of her encounter with the woman called—at that time—Caroline Franklin-Grout, it stuns me to see in Willa Cather herself the virtues of her characters. Flaubert is one of my favorite writers, and I'm equally enthusiastic about his correspondence and his biography. In his actions and letters, he always showed considerable affection for the daughter of his adored sister, who'd died during childbirth. But, because of the bad business deals accrued by her first husband, which more or less led Flaubert to ruin, because the writer never stopped having a thousand reasons for tormenting himself on her behalf and because the Goncourts had bandied about a variety of despicable acts they attributed to her, I'd always considered Caroline an impediment to Flaubert, yet another mishap that wasted a life for him that I am almost ready to believe was as flat, uneventful, grim and disappointing as he claims.

On the other hand, meeting the old lady, Willa Cather reinterprets everything in the opposite sense. In that octogenarian of 1930 who has read Proust (even if she finds him "*trop dur et trop fatigant*")[1] and adores Ravel, Scriabin and Stravinsky and has a face that grows younger as she listens to opera, Cather sees as

1. Translator's Note: "too hard and too tiring."

successful the education—"le goût des occupations intel-lectuelles"[2]—Flaubert wanted to give his niece, sees him as benefitting from someone equipped with a marvelous under-standing of him. "Could any situation be happier for a man of letters? How many writers have found one understanding ear among their sons or daughters?" Willa Cather cites a letter from Flaubert to Caroline whose words seem to her a perfect match for the old lady: "Un peu d'orthographe ne te nuirait,' pas, mon bibi! car tu écris *aplomb* par deux *p*: 'Moral et physique sont d'applomb,' trois *p* marqueraient encore plus d'énergie! Ça m'a amusé, parce que ça te ressemble."[3] Flaubert, she continues, had more than a companion in Caroline during his entire life—he had a "daughter of the house" to cherish and protect; and she, for her part, stored up his entire existence while close to her uncle, up to the handkerchief she used to wipe the perspiration from the writer's brow a few moments before his death.

Books protect me. I can always curl up well sheltered by them, as if they erected another universe entirely cut off from the real world. I have the paradoxical feeling that nothing can reach me there, whereas they also overwhelm me in an unhealthy way. I'm victimized by an excessive sensitivity to writing, like those forced to let their nails grow to avoid distractedly touching—I don't know what—when their fingers are just too fragile to stand the slightest contact. I, as well, should read with my fingernails but am too happy about being ceaselessly undermined.

I had tears in my eyes, an emotion that went over the top, as I read about that Flaubertian encounter. It's as if I recognized

2. Translator's note: "the taste for intellectual occupations."
3. Translator's note: "A bit of spelling wouldn't hurt you, my pet! since you write *aplomb* with two *p*'s; 'The mental and physical are balanced [*d'applomb*],' three *p*'s would signal even more energy! It amused me, because it's so you."

myself in Willa Cather and in Caroline at the same time, identified with their meeting. Since my father was the publisher of Samuel Beckett, Alain Robbe-Grillet, Claude Simon, Marguerite Duras, Robert Pinget, Pierre Bourdieu and Gilles Deleuze, I was familiar with several of those authors now recognized as the great ones. When I was still living at my parents', my father once asked if I kept a diary. It was more of an exhortation than an interrogation. No, pretension prevented me from keeping one, just as my father must have known. I'd decided to write and figured it would be too easy to go through that stage, attracting attention with a subject I didn't merit familiarity with, rather than with my astounding talent. My father, of course, wanted to help me and make my life easier, without worrying as well about my devotion, being assured that if I was writing such a book, I would submit it to him as editor so he'd be in a position to get rid of what displeased him; but at that moment, I was even surprised by the question, because I was so convinced he wouldn't have wanted me to reveal the slightest information for anything in the world. Even today, I'm more disposed to shamelessness than I am to indiscretion. But time has passed, my father is dead and for years I've thought it would show a minimum of generosity to fulfill the duty of writing a book about what I knew concerning admired writers as a way of pleasing some of their readers. Nevertheless, I can't find the right tone and don't know how to organize it, nor what to say and not say.

It's obvious that the greatest intimacy I'd had with both Michel Foucault and my father didn't exist for nothing. I was intensely close to Michel for a full six years, until his death, and I lived in his apartment for close to a year. Today I see that time as the period that changed my life, my cut-off from a fate leading me to the precipice. In no specific way I'm grateful to Michel, without knowing for exactly what, for a better life. Gratitude is too sweet a feeling to carry around; you've got to get rid of it, and a book is the only honorable, committed way. Whatever the particular value of several of the characters in my story, each finds its equivalent in every civilization: the burden of a father's love on his son, the son's need to wait for someone with the power to portray it differently to him so he can finally understand what it consisted of. It takes time to understand what it means to love.

Willa Cather also recounts that Caroline, while admitting that the future at her age was a tiny bit uncertain, invited her to come see her in Antibes during her next trip and offered, in any case, to send her a souvenir of their meeting—a letter from Flaubert, perhaps. The American answered that she was not a collector and that autographed letters had no meaning for her. Then it was time to say goodbye to that octogenarian who'd been married twice and had said nothing about her husbands, as if her uncle had been the only important person in her life. The following November, in New Hampshire, Cather got a letter from Madame Grout that arrived in a deplorable state, open and almost destroyed. It was because Caroline had left it in the hands of an obscure bookseller on a small street in Paris where she must have discovered one of Cather's books and had written to her based on the assumption, Willa Cather supposes, that booksellers were still publishers as they'd been in her day. There was nothing left inside but a word from Caroline announcing she'd enclosed a letter of 1866 from Flaubert to George Sand, but the document had disappeared.

Taking her time in order to find words that wouldn't wound her correspondent, Willa Cather answered the following month, saying that Caroline's desire for her to possess a letter from her uncle had more meaning for her than actual possession of it. She heard nothing more about the old lady until the following February, when some friends in Paris, who aren't identified, sent her the obituary of Mme Franklin-Grout, who had conserved, according to the article, "until an extremely advanced age, the intelligence and cheerful kindliness of a witty lady of society."

I'm not attached to autographs, either, even though Michel's wish for me to possess his hasn't compensated for my lacking it today. I have no fetish links to him. I like to talk about him, but not necessarily about his books. I was brought up not to annoy authors with their texts, not to infringe upon my father's prerogatives. What was obviously a pure delight for them with him would have been a chore with me. And, actually, I had no particular question to ask them; if I'd spoken to them it would have only been to tell them of my enthusiasm for reading, an often-awkward task that I usually renounced through a mixture of deference, laziness, cowardice and the values of a good education. I had no ambition to solve the great problems of the world by speaking with Michel nor was I trying to store up memories. I spoke to him about myself, and he tackled the question as if it were one of the great problems of the world. Life, sometimes, does merit reflection.

My father had the spirit of competition, and that degree of combativeness found its way into human relationships. When he told me the fantastic story of his connections with his publishing company, he spoke about always fighting alone, or almost, against everybody, or nearly. After his death, from various sources I learned that my grandfather had actually been of great help, and especially that he was the one who had had the idea of Jérôme becoming a publisher. Since I think such a profession is rarely chosen when it isn't hereditary, I saw the idea as so inventive and based on such a good knowledge of my father that I was moved by what it showed about my grandfather's love. Believing my father's stories, which I sadly view today as also serving to curb my attachment to my grandfather (as if there were some slight risk he'd overstep what I felt for my father), I always had reservations when it came to my grandfather and resented him for not having been more supportive of my father when he needed it. And here I was discovering that he had been, but his being dead for more than ten years meant that it was too late to adjust my affection for him.

"I've never met anyone so intelligent or so generous; it can't be by chance." For years, at times, I've daydreamed a storybook tale for which that sentence serves as turning point. I imagine a teenager or young man foundering in bitterness at a state orphanage or in prison, then encountering a man come to speak to the group he's part of—delinquent or abandoned children—a man who so affects the boy that he's freed, his discovery expressed in those few words. His life is changed as he is led away from resentment, building him a new, more confident existence, like a less dramatic remake of the adventures of Bishop Myriel and Jean Valjean. Fantastically, I've imagined myself as the instrument of that proactive kindness until, decades afterward, I've realized I'm its recipient, and it's Michel who has played that role for me.

My father loved and respected Samuel Beckett, the friend of his adult life, as he loved and respected no one. The day when he announced to me that Sam was dead, news that needed to be kept secret until the funeral, as he walked me to the door after I'd come for lunch, I offered him my condolences as simply as I could and, with his sad smile, he mentioned Michel by way of a response, to demonstrate that I knew how such things felt. Aware of the high esteem in which he held Sam and their friendship, which could very well have been the best he had, I was touched by such generosity. Not to be outdone by the gesture, I replied that for me it had only lasted six years (for him, it was about forty), although I wasn't really convinced that having enjoyed such an opportunity all his life was worse than seeing it prematurely interrupted. He offered another silent smile.

Ten or so years later, speaking about something completely different—new problems at work—my father told me, "Time used to be an ally and has become an enemy." "Time that sees all has found you out against your will,"[4] is the sentence with which Robbe-Grillet endows Sophocles in the epigraph to *The Erasers* (*Les Gommes*), a book so important in the career of "Monsieur le Directeur," as Alain called my father when I was a kid. And I've expanded the meaning of his own sentence beyond the professional context of my father, who I didn't know had barely a month more to live.

One afternoon, when I'd come to see my father and was speaking to him as he lay completely conscious in what would become his deathbed a few weeks later, he suddenly told me to leave him and attend to my own tasks. I refused by arguing that it was costing me nothing to be there; in fact, I was happy about it. He put a stop to this with that famous timid smile of his for acknowledging receipt of a compliment or kindness. But I insisted with the words, "because I love you," and when they were barely out of my mouth, I was glad I'd said them. My mother and sister, who were nearby, heard me and must have found my declaration appropriate enough for each of them to come and say, "I love you." Regardless of the circumstances, such effusion is hardly characteristic of our family. The words came to me naturally, although it was the first time I was expressing them to this particular person; but to the same extent, I thought they seemed irrelevant when spoken by others, right after mine, leaving me ill at ease and prompting me to leave the apartment a few minutes later, contradicting my previous declaration. Objectively, there was nothing about my mother's and sister's behavior to produce such an effect, even if an accumulation of affection like that

---

4. Translator's Note: Wording from the Richard Howard translation of the novel: *The Erasers* (Grove Press, 1964).

could pass for a deficit in tact that augured something sinister; yet merely a bit more refinement would have been enough to perceive that my own words were already inferring such a risk. On the other hand, I myself had no particular desire to love my father more than my mother and sister did—differently, yes, and I saw him a lot less than they did—but I don't think any jealousy could have caused me that feeling of unease. And yet, there it was.

Obviously, there was a lack of grace in my part of it. He'd left a posthumous letter for each of us, and my sister handed me mine the evening of his death. My father had written almost five years earlier:

> A few days before my father died, I was alone with him in his room at Ambroise-Paré, and I wanted to thank him for all he'd done for me since I came into the world. I have always known that I owed the least bad things about myself to those who'd brought me up and educated me, and to those whom I'd had the luck to meet after. And my father was obviously first in line for my gratitude. But I said nothing. Evidently, I feared that broaching a subject as intimate as that would only seem like wanting to make things right just before he died, a moment he may not have known was so close—although I doubt it. I kept silent and haven't regretted it since. What would he have done with my thank you's as he passed away? And yet, thinking about that unspoken admission is what gave me the desire to write to you before it is too late. When you read this letter, I'll have passed away as well, but you'll have a lot more years before you. Also, I believe that the gratitude I thought I did not have to show my father is completely appropriate to offer you.

I still have tears in my eyes as I recopy those lines. I'd said nothing a few weeks earlier that he didn't already know. What is more, despite his reserve and my tendency to believe that everyone detests me, I've never suffered from the slightest lack of affection on his part. I felt sure of it. In telling him, "I love you," I was only repeating a familial scene spanning the generations, and doing it with less delicacy than him. It still moves me that Sam and Michel haunt these lines, Sam in "those whom I'd had the luck to meet after"; Michel, because my father's words are so convincing that I can adopt them as mine—all those words, since, although I don't have a child, I still have the good luck of having someone to bequeath my gratitude. If I find myself in that fortunate situation, it's because I knew Michel and he changed my path. In his own way he, too, gave me life. At my father's bedside, wasn't I trying to "make things right"? And not with him, but with Michel, even if I hope that he nonetheless understood what I never said to him. Doesn't my unease have to do with the fact that from my perspective my mother and sister saying "I love you" to my father interferes with Michel, who was nothing to them? What absurdity has led to this feeling? Despite all the love in my family, I might never have been able to know Michel, never have been able to set foot in his apartment; and, despite all the love in my family, I pity the life I would have had.

For some time, I can't stop hearing the refrain from *À la Claire fontaine* in my head. "Il y a longtemps que je t'aime, jamais je ne t'oublierai."[5] Sometimes, it echoes through me with an icy tone. There is a way to pronounce it that sounds like a price to pay. "I've loved you for too long a time, and my vengeance will be eternal. For too long have you held me in chains, it doesn't matter how, or with which weapons. It doesn't matter whether it's reciprocal, whether it's happiness, it's been for too long." The never-ending "love-hate" relationship. I habitually see time as capital in emotional relationships—you could say that in my case

---

5. Translator's Note: "I've loved you for a long time, I'll never forget you."

I see it as a potential enemy. I'm someone who so loves to prolong love, to install its brutality in sweetness and its anxieties in serenity. When love hardens, is it still love? When it has finally become the best thing in the world.

I've wanted to write a book about Michel for too long, about our love and its endless ramifications, instead of claiming this refrain as mine. Of course, I'll never forget him—I'll always forget him—because now the magic is concentrated only in moments, reminiscences, and I alone am left to feed the relationship.

I want to pay tribute to him, but how to do it with a book, for someone whose own books can pay a thousand times more tribute than others would know how to do? He changed the life of thousands of people, but I know him for a fact, know him in a very specific way. There has been a man in my life for such a long time, more than a man—one of those men you want to show you deserve. A man so unusual he can't be used as an example, a man who is dead whom I loved and still love, who can serve as love—and what does love serve? A man with a wonderful apartment.

I was twenty-three and he raised me. To educate children we should always wait until they aren't, until they're old enough to have their own ideas; and such an inevitable handicap puts a strain on any relationship with parents who have always loved their child, always had him at their disposal. Michel educated me with such absolute discretion that I didn't know what I was learning. To be happy, alive. And gratitude.

I would have never loved Michel so much if he hadn't had that wonderful apartment. How can such a thing, which surely is the truth, be believed?

When my father survived a serious operation, my mother told me, "I'm grateful to him for not being dead," and I'd recounted this quip to Michel, who had found it lovely. Do I hold it against him for being dead? It's still the only fault I find in him, but it's a big one.

"Il y a longtemps que tu m'aimes, jamais tu ne m'oublieras"[6]: all you need do is reverse the sentence to grasp its potential for aggression. I've forgotten a thousand moments with him, but there are a thousand others I remember; and, obviously, I'll never forget him, he who even taught me death, incurable mourning, taught me without wanting to. Even so, I'm not going to be as thankful to him for that. He taught me life; there was no hurry for death. I wasn't yet thirty, but I believed he was going to continue to enrich my existence forever. Even though having known him was a great opportunity, the greatest was knowing him.

To talk about forgetting is to talk about love. "Did you think of me?" is always a moving question. I'm touched when loving doesn't have the absolute sense of a romantic relationship, when you love without sexuality or exclusivity, when Barbara sings that "there are people I love, in Göttingen, in Göttingen," or Jacques Brel sings in "*Mon père disait*," "The north wind will make me captain of a breeze of tears for a loving friend."[7] Has it been necessary to forget so that the dead who've been gone for a quarter of a century won't seem old-fashioned? Do memories live a new life when they're recruited for a text, like those characters in a novel who want to escape their creator to lead an independent life?

The last sentence of my father's posthumous letter is: "I only hope that when the time comes, I'll have the feeling that I've never caused you any serious harm, which will give me the right to ask you, as I kiss you, to forget me."

---

6. Translator's Note: "You've loved me for a long time, you'll never forget me."
7. From the song "Mon père disait" ("My Father Would Say"), which I've tried to rhyme like the original:
C'est le vent du nord
Qui me fera capitaine
D'un brise-larmes
Pour ceux que j'aime

ENCOUNTERS

"We": I'm not aware that the word is in use outside the family. Encountering somebody is a feat. I don't know how to attach those who aren't in my life to it. A lack of function creates the absence of an organ, and it's as if I don't even desire its necessity. I have no place in the world, then, like my father's fighting spirit. Such an obvious fact pertains to every element of my life: I'm the only one who wants to have friends, make love. Reciprocity isn't imaginable. To think that every relationship would be a conquest, a wrestling hold on an enemy, whose consent you've got to rip out by force or skill, a dishonest compromise with the real. I have no strategy, no social guerilla's manual to learn how to extricate myself from that jungle, so I give up, allowing chance to come into it, which I'm careful not to provoke. For my happiness and my unhappiness, I love to read, and solitude is a friend who saves me the trouble of looking for them in others.

1

After an adolescence that has been as endless as it was disastrous, I suddenly meet a human being. It starts with a girl. I invite her to my room in my parents' home where I still live, and she's surprised when I get explicit, notices a brutality that is my only way not to be anesthetized by reserve and refinement. Yes, she's surprised, and willing. Very quickly, I'm in love, and that's a decision, certainly, because love is a strategy. It's giving yourself heart and soul and going for broke, learning confidence. I'm so controlled in every way that passion is the only weapon I have left. Nothing can be resolved if not by outburst, scattering my prejudices and other defenses like a puzzle. I hold onto that. I've read too many books during my hellish adolescence. I've seen too many films and listened to too many songs not to have my own idea of love. Valérie is beautiful, intelligent, likeable—presentable to my parents—how couldn't she be desirable? An acceptable object for my passion going by at heart's reach—I throw myself on top of her.

I'm in luck, if only for the fact that this girl openly takes lovers, one-night stands, a situation that contradicts novels of classic love. I'm ashamed of suffering and causing scenes. In principle, I too am an advocate of promiscuity, but the very definition of love is its great distance from theory to practice.

Until now, it's as if life has been slipping through my fingers, as if it were only a bad moment to go through. As if, with enough prudence, precaution and inertia, it's possible to keep it at a distance and arrive safe and sound at the moment when there will no longer be anything to choose—or live. It's a radical form of paranoia: life as an enemy with whom I can still negotiate provided I don't ask anything of it. You have to let sleeping dogs lie, so if I stay very quiet and don't move, nothing will happen to me, strictly nothing. But who knows if the dog isn't a better companion awake than asleep? Impossible to avoid that question by opposing it with will. It floats back up to the surface. That's how love pries open your appetite; youth is a dog with insomnia.

One evening, as I'm walking to Valérie's apartment, a teenager comes up to me and asks what time it is. By the time I tell him, I'm surrounded by four or five other boys who now want my money. They aren't crazy: the street is too empty for me to be able to call anyone for help. Or maybe I should have screamed to make my aggressors run, an act of resistance that would alert people who live on the street rather than anyone passing by. I give them my money. Then one of the boys demands my watch. It's a family heirloom that means a great deal to me, and I bargain.

"Oh no," I begin.

I get ready to tell them that it's only because I had the politeness to answer a request to know the time that I've ended up in this situation, and that it would be a bitter irony if I have to pay more for that courtesy with the watch I adore. Indignation, suddenly, has surpassed my fear.

"That'll do," says one of the boys, not to me but to his buddies, and the aggressors disappear on their mopeds, not so much convinced by my argument, which they hadn't fully heard, as having become afraid themselves, since they're more teenagers than professionals.

I continue walking to the apartment, climb the flights with a beating heart, explain to my lover, who'd immediately noticed how livid I was, why I'm in such a state. That this happened on my way to her place is an added cruelty, as if I had good reasons to stay home alone at my place since the imbecilic adolescent I was—shut up reading day and night—had carefully weighed the pros and cons. I'm totally unaware of where I am, lost, the lowest of the low, not morally but literally speaking. Very quickly, however, I find my way back to the fact that I couldn't be happier to be here. Valérie knows what to do about it, and I understand that she doesn't at all see me as lost, some kind of mental vagrant, a sort of social madman without a future, which is exactly what I've feared since adolescence, something the mugging makes seem even truer to me, adding an aspect that no longer has any fantasy element to it.

"You're different from the others," she says. She's younger than me, but bolstered by experience and her familiarity with so many boys. "Nobody knows what he's going to do with his life. But you want to write."

I had no idea of any privilege, anything I can imagine inspiring jealousy. I'd have to be happier than I am. How can I make my girlfriend understand that, even though I might be a future writer, I'm expecting something other from life than books?

***

I suggest I go with Valérie to a film about a woman who is raped and every facet of the after-effects she experiences as a result. It's something being discussed a lot at this moment, the film intending to trigger society to become aware of the extent of a tragedy that has been under-evaluated.

"No," she says. "It's going to turn you on."

I don't insist. I don't know what there is about my sexual behavior that leads my girlfriend to believe such a thing. But it's true. I'd be less enthusiastic about seeing a film on racism or battered children. I expect more satisfaction out of rape. As a teenager, at a ski camp, I ended up in a room with four boys who were having fun finding nicknames for each of us. For example, one of them called himself Obsex, short for "Sexual Obsessive," because he was always talking about girls and what he'd do with them. A rule of the game was that, to be accepted, the nickname had to get the votes of a majority of those who were there, including the person to whom the name referred. That was the case for Obsex. When my turn came to be named, Obsex suggested Trobsex, short for "Very Sexually Obsessed" ("*Très obsédé sexuel*"), which was that much more surprising from the fact that no one could rightfully criticize or congratulate me for speaking in an exaggerated way about girls or what was done with them. Another boy immediately spoke up and voted against it. Even so, I accepted it. "In that case, I take back my vote," said the boy who had thought he was defending me by being against the name. As for me, I was still a virgin, and the fact that I was weighed on me like a bad mark, a guilt-inspiring ignorance. I associated being linked to sex with an advantage, even if it was obsessively or out of proportion. It was better than nothing.

Something of that nature is connected to rape. I've never raped anyone and certainly wouldn't like to do it or have it happen to me. However, I have nothing against that act as a fantasy. Sometimes I'm thinking of it during sex, perfectly assured as I am of my partners' consent, which is the real stipulation that makes it easy for me to create such make-believe. I think I'd never be able to rape anyone for real, and that the blood would drain from my penis at the slightest resistance or the slightest disapproval more or less tacitly expressed during coitus, creating a profound mixture of physical and psychological impotence. Since I'm already often stifled with my partners by replaying that first time with each when I was worried about not letting them down despite myself, and since by the second time a guarantee has already been given, if only just to myself, making my mind feel freer, the absolutely novel charm of a peaceful taking of virginity— if that is what they call each first time—has partly faded and seems out of reach like too much fine-tuning. Rape fires up my mind, but not my body.

A film represents the ideal. It would offer me new images of rape that are more concrete than those I invent even if they are less exactly matched to me, not to mention that what you see in a film is feigned. Psychology doesn't have to get mixed up in it.

I like the tone Valérie used to keep me from going to the movies with her; it wasn't hostile, just pure observation. If she's interested in rape, it has nothing to do with getting excited about it. She merely prefers not to see the film with someone whose motives are too different, just as two people aren't encouraged to watch a soccer game when each supports a different team.

I go to dinner with Valérie after she gets out of the theater, and she tells me she wasn't wild about the film. Afterward we go back to her place and have sex. I don't think it's necessary to modify what goes through my mind at the most select moments. Instead I feel I've received full acquittal for my inner narrative. I don't wonder how my partner is interpreting that, assured as I am of the secret in my brain when it's obvious that even Valérie's refusal to share seeing the film with me indicates that she's some-what aware of what I was thinking. It's just the same when drug addicts spend an hour shooting up in the toilet and think they're doing it secretly, whereas everyone knows what they're up to in there. Believing in a secret is enough to make it one.

"That was great," I say, to have something to say after coming.

"Yes," she answers. "You see, don't worry about it."

2

I meet Valérie's lovers with a favorable bias. If she thinks these boys are worthy of being her partners, they must certainly deserve it. Marc, her former lover, becomes my close friend. One evening, we happen to go to bed together. It turns out well enough to make me want to repeat the pleasure a few days later. Marc avoids it. But two months later, Marc's the one who's ready to stay overnight at my place without my having offered. I turn him down. It riles me that the other person believes that my desire is permanent and that he has the right to have it so sporadically. We remain friends but, without my having really understood the meaning of my rebuff at that moment, sex doesn't come up again and that's o.k., too.

A boy who's exactly my age enjoys a special status in Valérie's group of friends because he has had a passionate relationship with Michel Foucault. At first such intimacy with someone so respected soured me toward Thierry, since I have known so many famous authors without having ever attained a comparable familiarity with them. However, I'd seen him from the time I'd first known Valérie, and the boy's beauty, his hair falling to his shoulders the way I like it, had immediately changed my mind, and I had been heartbroken about not ending the night with him. "He didn't understand that you wanted him," Valérie told me the next day, having gotten information about him in order to console me.

Thierry belongs to a group of revolutionaries and, unlike the boys in that gang or myself, hasn't gotten himself declared unfit for military service, hasn't even tried to. His organization was recommending they take advantage of their military service to spread the word to young people. He'd just become drafted when his group changed strategy and called for getting out of it. That hadn't bothered Thierry who, for lack of the revolution, had sex during his military service with a great variety of comrades and found a lot of gratification during that period. When I see him again, his hair is short, without it having ruined neither his beauty nor my desire. This time he has been clued in to my expectations. The affair happens, lasts. Meanwhile, Valérie seems completely in love with a new boy, making things go even better between us and keeping me benefitting from her sexual generosity.

Like all the people in Valérie's gang, Thierry is an anti-victim who turns everything that happens to him into an advantage, or at least a claimed one. One day when I say to him, "Even so, it would be better if God did exist. At least we could complain," he laughingly answers that only a Jew could say such a thing. Thierry comes from a strict Catholic family in the sixteenth arrondissement, in which his militant homosexuality creates such a fuss that Marc enjoys putting it into question by wondering if his parents' irritation is the main reason for his sexual orientation. Not wanting to receive any money from his family, Thierry, who is studying Japanese, also works evenings as a nurse's aide at the Hôtel Dieu hospital. I often come around midnight to wait for him for an hour, and we go back to spend the night together in his studio apartment, independent but adjoining the apartment belonging to Michel Foucault, who is loaning it to him. Thierry always has outrageous stories that he recounts humorously, although I can't figure out how true they are.

"You know the first sentence the majority of people in car accidents say when they come out of a coma?"

"No," I answer.

And he, who knows what he's talking about because of his hospital experience, which trains you to value caution, says, "But I had the right of way!"

That speaks to me. For me, as well, being right, the one who's correct, is a vital notion. I'm an accident victim of justice.

I find a logical justification in turning to people of my own sex even if that logic only has meaning for me, which is more than enough since I'm also the only one to call for an explanation: I'm jealous of Valérie's feeling sperm shooting up inside her, the wonderfully warm sensation it must be, seeing that she is taking the pill and that I therefore don't have any reason to wear a condom. There aren't a myriad of ways I can experience this little fleeting and personal geyser. The truth is that it doesn't work; the sperm I receive doesn't have the same effectiveness, but even so, there are other ways of being satisfied and other positions. I'm someone who's always afraid of not being good enough, who's constantly thinking about the need to prove myself, so I extend these anxieties to the partners I find. Do they deserve it? Turning to such boys involves no risk. It's almost no longer a choice. Their value has already been recognized by Valérie, whose worth I know. As a result, there's no shame in they're becoming my lovers and everything acquires an astonishing simplicity. Although relationships with girls were so complex, obviously I just don't value them. The fact that my partners are boys now has an originality that suits me. Homosexuality furnishes a bit of class. Too bad for my poor adolescence, when greater banality might have been more appropriate. It's behind me now. Welcome to the time of freedom, its happy and productive ups and downs. I'm getting back on the right track. Youth is about to end by being for me.

***

Someone's knocking. It's getting louder and louder, but it's the bell that manages to wake us up. It's two in the morning. I'm in bed with Thierry in the studio apartment loaned to him by Michel Foucault. We fell asleep easily after having made love.

"It's Gérard," says a voice behind the door.

Thierry gets up naked and opens the door.

I've already seen Gérard once, by chance, and he's the only one of Valérie's lovers with whom I'm familiar who didn't appeal to me very much. On the other hand, I know that his relationship with Thierry has been intensely intimate for years, one of those adolescent infatuations I've learned about only through reading. I thought Gérard had gone on a motorcycle trip around the world for months and months, and it's a surprise to see him here at this hour. In fact, the boy, who's tall—he must measure almost 6' 5"—has just gotten back from Afghanistan after more than a year there with Jean-Marie, Thierry's older brother in that family of six sons. Not knowing where to find Thierry, he simply came to see him at the apartment as soon as possible. As for the hour, he doesn't need to excuse himself; Thierry is so obviously happy to see him that it's clear no fault has been committed. The two of them talk and talk, completely delighted, not concerned about my presence. My double status as Valérie's lover and then Thierry's gives me implicit entry into the gang. It doesn't bother me, either, despite being woken up in the middle of the night. It changes my habits, which is never good, but perhaps it's where life is leading. No matter how careful you are, the unavoidable is always part of existence.

This is the first time I've slept naked with two others, but I do sleep, letting them keep talking. I get up earlier to go to work (through a family connection I've gotten an internship at the *Nouvel Observateur*) after all three of us have agreed to meet at my place with Valérie next Tuesday to watch a film on television that Gérard recommends.

Tuesday, neither Valérie nor Thierry show up. I'm alone at home with Gérard without feeling intimidated. Having slept naked in the same bed must help. Suddenly he's reaching into his own underpants from which he unpeels a band-aid to reveal some cargo that turns out to be opium brought back from Afghanistan. I've never taken any drug. I don't know anything about it and react with general panic at the most soft-core of such practices. Normally, I would flee the second I'm threatened by any drug at all that endangers my preciously acquired equilibrium. To my own amazement, I willingly accept. Gérard explains that the best thing to do, if you have the right kind of pipe, is to smoke the opium; but if not, it's possible to swallow it with a glass of water. You have to roll the drug between your fingers—on which it leaves a stain—into a solid pellet that water will wash down without difficulty if you don't tense up at the first swallow. It works. I'd never tasted anything like it until then; it has an acridity that corresponds to its consistency. Opium resembles nothing but opium. Such a hard drug is of an unsuspected softness, and we spend a marvelous night in the sensuality of bodies and emotions, filled with laughter. I leave Gérard at three in the afternoon, dazzled. We never even watched the film. From now on I'll never refuse the slightest crumb of opium.

Nor do I ever want to lose the slightest crumb of Gérard. We make love in the magnificence of opium, and these marvelous moments also have their radical uniqueness. It's as if sensuality were a world into which we merely have to glide, which we inhabit independently of our desire. We just followed the slope of our state. It doesn't happen again. After having observed that this interlude has caused no harm, Gérard, for whom homosexuality is not the strongest orientation, tells me about having feared that our friendship, which started off so well, would suffer from a physical imbalance. No. Mysteriously, my love for

Gérard doesn't have a lot to do with sexuality. That's why, I imagine, it's called friendship. This is something I've never known: an adolescent passion occurring with ten years of maturity, not to mention immaturity.

Gérard leaves me some opium that I take with another lover: a memorable night. Gérard also tells me about Afghanistan, the highs and lows he experienced with Thierry's brother during the trip, the return of each with opium, their pact to share the profits made by selling it. Gérard gave away all of his. Jean-Marie sold all of his but split the booty into two equal parts without complaining. I was afraid human relationships were more limited than that. This, as well, has opened up a world. Apparently, the bourgeoisie isn't universal.

***

Thierry's bed proves to be a site for encounters all its own. Sometimes, in the morning, he goes into the apartment adjoining the studio and connected by an invisible door at the side of the apartment (you'd think it was only the door to a closet) and then comes back to announce that breakfast for three is ready next door. Spending time with Michel Foucault is nothing less than a gift, especially since his appearance is somewhat—although not surprisingly—well meaning. However, I'm beginning to suspect that Thierry delays it on purpose. To help Thierry earn a little money, he put together a book with him (with his own contribution kept anonymous) containing conversations on being young, about what it's like to be twenty today. And I enjoy interviewing Thierry about his text for *Le Nouvel Observateur*, finding it more playful than unethical, despite the fact that I know the identity of the person who has the conversation with Thierry in the book. Michel rereads the interview and suggests a thousand corrections, all enthusiastically approved. When I submit the article to my department head, she accepts it condescendingly, detecting all the naiveties of people our age. That amuses me, as well. I don't believe in journalism.

Thierry and I are just two days apart in age. Recently we got into the habit of celebrating our birthdays by lunching together the day after one and the day before the other. When he comes to get me at the office of the magazine, Michel is with him. He invites us to the restaurant and then takes us to the opening of an exhibition at Beaubourg. In one of the corridors of the exhibition, Thierry, who has been walking ahead of us, returns to tell us that the attractive boy in front of us, but who is with a girl, has just told her he recognized Michel. The girl merely responded, "Who's Michel Foucault?" Thierry reports jubilantly. "An illiterate," quips Michel with that hearty laugh of his that is still inside me. And, strangely at ease, I'm having the feeling of living my own vital literacy campaign at top speed, of beginning to unravel the confusion of feelings.

We become friends. Michel, one evening when I've gone to dinner at his place with Gérard and Marc, suggests that I kiss him. The proposal unsettles me. For some mysterious reason, I find it brave to refuse with a single word, keeping my tongue well sheltered, braver than dissolving into tears or showing complete incomprehension, even though that's the dominant impression. Once again, I've been put on the spot. Thierry has certainly lived with Michel, so what would be so strange about my sleeping with him, or at least exchanging a few kisses? I've never thought about it, and not having done so is an argument against such an exchange, as if suddenly, any proposition, even a romantic or sexual one, called for a waiting period of reflection in the cold light of day. I have no pretensions about being as free-spirited as Thierry. I still need to calculate in one way or another, to protect myself by contract.

Once we've left Michel's apartment, I go back to that episode, staving if off with a proclaimed sense of pride. I flatter myself as if for honesty lacking any pretense, for the clarity of my "No," all the while strongly feeling that something is escaping me, running counter to me, hurting me. If not, then why am I talking about it again?

"You were ridiculous," Gérard says to me.

I'm convinced he means it, given the fact that he's never said a word against me and because Marc is remaining silent. Shame strikes me immediately. I'd take Michel in my arms and hold him tight, let him do the same, with all my heart. But it's too late.

It reminds me of the Sunday I was waiting in line in a good bakery with Gérard and the woman in front of us addressed the saleswoman in such a peculiar way that she told her people didn't talk to her in such a tone. The woman got furious and walked out, and I shared a reflection with Gérard that showed what camp I thought I belonged to, the satisfaction I felt in seeing what was uncouth punished that way.

"That was a lady who was thrilled to be eating some cakes on Sunday and who won't be," was all he answered.

The pleasure camp is one I ought to be in more often.

***

A naked Japanese dancer is performing at Michel's place, and Thierry and I are part of the guests. The nudity of the dancer is a special attraction, and although I really was invited to Michel's apartment by the owner himself, it's currently not a common occurrence. And there's something else that appeals to me. For weeks, Michel has been speaking to me about Hervé, a boy my age about whom I've been reading some astonishing articles in *Le Monde*, and he'll be there, too. Michel's sponsorship has removed any terror from this real-life meeting.

About ten of us are watching the show, all men, besides Thierry, Hervé and I, who are still only young men. The Japanese performance isn't very long, and then the naked dancer disappears to put his clothes back on. Various guests are commenting about his performance without it leading to any debate, while I keep my mouth shut because I don't know what to say, being as ignorant about dance as about Japan.

"But he wasn't really nude," someone suddenly says.

In fact, the dancer had only gotten down to a decent penile cover. And everyone gets going again discussing that less artistic observation, laughing about finally reaching the point of more serious things.

Next, each converses in his corner, except for Hervé, who remains conspicuously alone. Given the place and Michel's presence, I feel confident enough to be taken in the right way and I dare to come up to him while choosing my words. "Are you being punished, Hervé Guibert?" After that, we don't use the formal *vous* again. Hervé smiles, tells me five minutes later that he'll send me some texts for the literary review in which I'm involved as I've asked him to, already convinced as I am of their quality by the articles about him and by Michel's lobbying. I supposed I've benefitted from similar praise about me offered to Hervé. It would never have worked as well if not. We talk a few more minutes and leave the party early—Thierry and I because we're going to another dinner, Hervé because he prefers not to hang around with that small crowd. But I haven't lost any time: I'm in love already. I need at least that to get fired up.

Literature excites me. Hervé has a book published that I'm reading with enthusiasm, thinking nevertheless that it's useful, among my compliments, to express my reservations. I love the texts that he's giving me for my review. It's more than obvious this boy is up to snuff, leaving me free to get involved as much as I desire. The question of sex stops dead in its tracks. Fortunately, this friendship is a kind of love. We flirt until one evening Hervé, although in love with another, finally agrees to come home with me. A few steps from my studio, he changes his mind definitively and leaves me to spend the night alone. I'm irritated, but I catch the flu and, the next time Hervé calls, I have a 102-degree fever. I don't think of reproaches and only recount the complications I've been having with my lover of the moment, the main point being that I'm no longer wild about him. There's an immediate disappearance of the potential problems that come with sex, and we invent another kind of intimacy for ourselves. Being homosexuals without lovers is a way of life that brings us closer, and we now pass an infinite number of evenings together, hanging out after dinner in bars where we learn about each other's kind of desire—at whom it's directed and how each of us attempts to make something good out of it. I always look for the handsomest boy, whereas Hervé, so handsome himself, claims to be attracted to people seemingly less sexy whose advances he nevertheless refuses when on occasion they come on to him; and he always goes home alone after our evenings together. We laugh a lot, which is always essential in my relationship with another person, but for Hervé it's something new, which brings us even closer.

One evening, I am urgently requisitioned for a dinner. Hervé has invited Michel and Daniel to his place. Daniel is Michel's boyfriend, who is younger than him but even so mostly an adult and not ordinarily comparable with us. Hervé has never before used his studio to entertain, and all of a sudden, he's nervous about the possibility and asking me to come. It happens at the right time: I was just supposed to have dinner with Thierry who will be an extra reinforcement. We're a bit tense, so proud of our friendship with Michel that we're afraid to make the slightest mistake. Thierry is late because he's involved in the creation of *Gai Pied*,[1] a gay weekly whose name Michel has thought of, and the release of the first issue needs some work. Thierry arrives with this treasure in hand that no one has yet been able to see. Thanks to him there is a text by Michel in it that, obviously, is announced on the front page. "But that's not the right title," says Michel, not managing entirely to hide his feelings when he sees the cover. No one knows where to sit, and there's an uneasiness that lasts all evening, although Michel had skillfully stopped himself the second he noticed the bad effect of his remark. There won't be any more dinners at Hervé's place. When we talk on the telephone the next morning, he mentions his failure in order to be consoled and I, who was too anxious the night before to notice his chosen strategy, fully agree with him, like an idiot, and he makes fun of me. And I'm fine with that because I like him, because our relationship pleases me just as it pleases him, and because, since Valérie, after going through adolescence alone, I have been miraculously carried away as if it's no big deal into a ceaseless maelstrom of affection.

---

1. Translator's note: A pun in French: *gai* = "gay"; *pied* = "foot." However, a *guêpier*, pronounced similarly as the two words combined, means "trap" or "wasp's nest" and suggests the well-known idiom *se fourrer dans un guêpier* = "to land oneself in the soup."

3

"Do you feel something?" says Gérard.

"No, maybe the coffee a little," I say, while sniffing to get a better idea. "I'm waiting for you outside," I add as I walk out of the store.

We're spending a week of vacation in New York, where Gérard has a good friend, a girl named Immy, who gave us some LSD that we took three quarters of an hour ago. The question has to do with the effect of the drug that I ingested trustfully but actually didn't know anything about—for me it's the first time, and I don't know what's going to happen. When Gérard finds me a minute later, I'm lying spread out full length on Broadway and people are stopping to ask if I'm o.k. Surprised that they think it makes sense to speak to me, I answer *yes* (in English) with an enormous smile. The entire day is a miracle, a mental and emotional explosion that enlarges my horizons. As planned, we take a taxi to join Immy in Central Park at Seventy-second Street, but we don't manage to indicate the address for the driver—"sixty douze," "seventy deux," "sixty-twelve"—we get caught up in confusion and laugh and then laugh at our laughter. Despite all this, we manage to arrive at the right place, and from all evidence we're first, so we look for a comfortable spot to sit. We've barely chosen a patch of grass to sit on when we get back up, because the grass next to it is greener and thicker; but as soon as we move, the new place won't do either, because the grass farther away is even better; and we continue this endless migration until we realize that our angle of vision is what makes the difference—the grass is the same everywhere.

Immy takes us to an apartment equipped with a lavish bathroom. Both of us sit down at one end of the big tub and turn the water on, letting it run in an attempt to find the most suitable temperature. And that goes on forever as well because it's too hot and we add cold water, and then it's too cold and we add hot water, and then it's perfect but it gets cold from the loss of heat and our getting used to it. We laugh buckets, producing a much greater feeling of well being than what the water and its temperature are likely to bring. We're looking for an ideal balance—the acid demands that we do.

Michel's apartment is miraculously the concretization of that ideal. We know it because taking acid keeps on there. Its space and its layout make it a dream place for that kind of pleasure. We take a thousand precautions. Gérard has told me a lot of stories, the risk of everything getting out of hand, the possibility of the situation becoming as horrible as it can be marvelous, and it's perfectly understood that if one of us at the last moment prefers not to take the drug, he won't incur the slightest protest. There are four of us, Marc, Gérard, Michel and I, and no one turns it down. All of us describe the acid coming on—it requires about an hour after taking it for the effect to begin to become pronounced—except in my case, since I'm not experienced and only perceive the changes when they're so advanced it's impossible to deny them. There's a corner of the apartment against the picture window, next to the record player, where we gather on four armchairs with cushions while listening to Mahler's first symphonies. That music has an element of the fairground to it, and this added to its high quality perfectly matches the violent sweetness of the paradisiacal moments. There's no greater teacher than LSD to turn you into a music lover, and you live that music intensely. The comedown from the acid is less pleasant, and we sit around a bit irritated while rediscovering our old consciousness, which closely resembles melancholy. But this additional intimacy enchants all four of us.

We're better prepared for the next session. Gérard has gotten hold of some opium to smooth the coming down from the LSD. Also, both of us have gone and rented a projector, a screen and two films—one for the acid and one for the opium—which we bring to the apartment. We're the same four as last time, and once more I'm the last to recognize the feeling of getting off as we again listen to Mahler. Next we move on to the film with the Marx Brothers. Only we've made the mistake of not having set up the screen and, especially, the projector with the first reel before the showing, which is to take place at the other end of the apartment in the studio where Thierry lived. Marc, gifted with a sense of the practical, is trying to do it, but that initiates a spell of nuttiness during which we laugh our heads off, our state of mind making it unlikely to pull off this kind of technical manipulation. After the film, which is a hit, there's a game of Pick-Up Sticks on the living room carpet. It's very difficult to play anything at all during an acid trip because you can't ever be sure of keeping the rules in your head or of using them to be a good arbiter, and should you really trust your hallucinating eyes? Never have laughter and meticulousness been so combined. When it's my turn to play, I bend over backward to do it well, as to me it seems a moral test that, far from wanting to escape, I'm exceptionally happy to confront. Consequently, I think I'm showing myself under my best light and am stunned when Michel says, "There, that's enough," with the evident agreement of Gérard and Marc. Apparently, without my realizing it, the sticks have moved as much as they can for a long time. But what signifies a long time when temporal distortions are added to visual ones? A second later, we're laughing like druggies.

The idea of the opium is inspired because it avoids having to put up with a sort of energy you no longer know what to do with after acid. Given the fact of how strong LSD is, you would willingly go to sleep if you didn't feel so tense; but instead of that, we slip little by little into a strange softness, the extraordinary mental activity of the past moments mutating into an unexpected serenity. One of us is homosexual and in his fifties—with three young men, two of whom are heterosexual. Nothing feels oppressive, even for me. However, Gérard's favorite film, which we watch during our first opium session after acid, is *Citizen Kane*; and it's especially moving and successful in these circumstances. After the showing, I talk to Michel in the big room and he sings the praises of the old friend of Orson Welles played by Joseph Cotton; whereas I play the smartass and act the cynic with whom you can't get away with such things. I defy how I'm really feeling and say that the character's diehard moral stance has a pain-in-the neck aspect, as if I tend never to trust virtue, whereas in truth I adore it in this instance. A beautiful life is like the one Joseph Cotton is portraying. Next, I'm afraid there's been a misunderstanding that has falsely reduced my image in Michel's eyes, the same one I just pieced together. But losing our minds and discovering others, recycling ones from the past—for us it's all good. Nor is our respect for Michel a drawback. Sharing acid is a relationship of a superior order in itself, inaccessible to most. Michel is always peerless, and from that perspective, drugs have no effect on him.

4

"And since you've decided never to marry," my father says to me at one point as we're discussing some indeterminate subject in his office at éditions de Minuit. Such a conversation is rare because our shyness increases and in general my father is rarely so free with words, skillfully demonstrating this or that point while keeping personal elements from interfering in our relationship as much as he can. He's a master of conversation, always able to cash in on the slightest phrase you grant him.

I don't react to the words forecasting my bachelorhood, which haven't changed my feeling that I haven't decided yet. The same evening I quote them to Michel at whose home I'm dining. It's my attempt to demonstrate the independence from my father I'm finally achieving, and in this case, specifically, that I have no trouble apprehending the imprecise nature of my father's remark. To my surprise, Michel fully agrees with him, making me understand that my non-decision is a decision, and that those who'll marry start organizing the framework of their lives very early on, whereas I easily admit, for example, never having imagined having children. Similarly, I haven't decided not to work with my father in his publishing house, seeing that for years and years it has felt like an obvious corollary of belonging to my family—not to mention the fact that I look after a review there and spend every Sunday afternoon in those offices reading the texts that have been sent and responding to them. I can in any case grab hold of this net after a failure, and since there will always be time to do so, I'm at least choosing to try other work and discover some small something in the outside world and the population inhabiting it, like an agoraphobic shut up in his room who one day, in fair weather, courageously tries going out just to its entrance. I understand nothing about what's happening inside me, and at present I'm still full of such schizophrenic perplexity.

From the start I have no respect for this occupation of journalist I'm trying out at the *Nouvel Observateur* through an internship not subject to any fixed period of time. My father's contempt for the media and for the kind of publishing he doesn't practice has been strong enough to contaminate me. The fact that such apparent hostility could be a strategy, a manifestation of his constant taste for competition, never enters my mind. My own contempt is real. The first times I go to the *Nouvel Observateur*, I'm surprised about having to deal with human beings, certainly with their faults, but also with their skills, which are no less evident. For me, however, the real world is still an ideal world of literature—it's despite everything that, kicking and screaming, I go slumming in another, only because life demands going through that stage. One day at the magazine we want to contact Marguerite Duras because she has just experienced something unusual and it would be good to have the scoop of her commentary. It's being suggested I call her. We're in the middle of a packed meeting in the director's office, and never before have I taken the floor. I react like an idiot who hasn't grasped the fact that the reason for the request is precisely because Marguerite Duras has just experienced something exceptional, which of course she's in no mood to talk about, and if she did, it would be only because it was me calling and therefore, I myself add with twisted reasoning, it wouldn't be right to call. "Such scruples do you honor," says Jean Daniel, provoking the others' laughter to such an extent that it becomes obvious they should quickly stifle it. I resolve to telephone Marguerite Duras, but the way I transmit the request presents it as more or less ridiculous and myself as shameful for being its messenger, anticipating her refusal to such an extent that she can't do other than refuse. I wouldn't have forgiven myself or my father for mixing the worlds of media and literature so crudely.

Becoming part of the magazine is a crucial task although, if my father hadn't spoken to me about it, I would never have imagined such work, nor any other. In any case, I'll write, even if I do know better than anyone—having heard it so often—that there's no money to be earned in that business, that no writer can count on it. I'm so certain of being too intelligent for one thing or too stupid for another that there's no place for me anywhere unless I'm clever enough to succeed in tricking everyone around me. On the other hand, I'm so used to being bored that any activity amuses me, which makes me a more pleasant colleague.

Finding myself a film critic, I have the strong suspicion that my opinion about the films I see counts, and at the same time that I'm not misjudging my competences. As Michel and Hervé are also very often invited to screenings and since each can come with somebody, we arrive as a group at times, and Michel, pointing to me, may say to the flabbergasted publicist who immediately recognizes him that he's with his gang. Conversely, he has already shouted out to me from one end of the hall to the other to ask me if it wasn't boring me to be a critic, since I'm no big fan of films, and that delights me, too. One day Hervé and I see an Italian film together, which I find the lowest of the low and Hervé adores. Michel goes back to it with him and then tells me about having been put in the position to like the film that, however, very quickly bored him to death; and at the end, when he'd tried to say something favorable, Hervé cut him short by remarking he'd detested the work from the first moment of that second viewing. And we laugh at that assortment of opinions, as we do about the desserts in a restaurant where I often dine with Hervé and from where you leave so fat you imagine only being able to get home by rolling. My opinion being scorned doesn't bother me a whit, it amuses me—even as if it had nothing to do with me—and it has no influence on me in any way nor on the affection in which I'm held. How reassuring.

By his profession and the way he exercises it, my father attaches the greatest value to his own opinions, and he's happy that others—with me first in line—agree with them as much, if not more. One evening when I tell Michel about my admiration for Boileau[1] and his nastiness, he answers that he himself doesn't like him, and particularly, if I understand, for the way posterity has substantiated his judgments, as if he'd turned out to be the avant-garde of literary correctness. In a film festival at Hyères where the magazine sends me, a woman writer whom I don't know very well because she is published by another press says to me, when she knows who my father is, that he's the most cautious man she knows. I myself tend to see him as the bravest, but she has spoken without ill will, which convinces me that there is no opposition between the two points of view. Because I've begun exposing myself to people who aren't from the family, my cult for my father and all the cultural symbolism attached to it are suddenly encountering reality.

---

1. Translator's note: Nicolas Boileau-Despréaux (1636–1711), French poet and critic who reformed French poetry by satire and example. Devoted to demolishing books he thought stupid, he attacked several of the most highly praised writers of his time, many of whom, as he expected, are not well known today.

RUE DE VAUGIRARD

1

Looking back, I can't get over it: when Michel announces to me that he will leave Paris for two months of the summer and suggests I stay in his apartment during that time, he presents it as a favor that I'm doing him—the plants on the balcony need watering daily—and immediately I accept. Such a new approach, however, isn't really my thing. I'll have to believe the apartment is already living inside me. It's a bigger, more luxurious, but not better one. Inhabiting it is inhabiting youth itself.

It is made up of an immense room more than thirty feet long, bordered by a picture window that supplies it with a great deal of light since it's on the ninth floor without anything opposite. At one end of that enormous space is the Mahler corner with the armchairs into which we burrowed with a blanket on the days we took acid, turning it into what we called our nest because it evoked such homey comfort. Then, not separated by any wall is what could properly be called the living room, with the couch in front of the library, opposite which are some equally comfortable armchairs, located on the other side of a low coffee table and still leaving a lot of space until the picture window because the width of this room is just as impressive. On a pillar near the couch are hung three photos of Daniel, Michel's companion, laughing and looking happy—love photos in the same way you use that word with *songs*, images of contagious joy. The living room continues along with what is also an extension of the library, which is stuffed with books. It's a kind of office that can be closed off by a detachable partition but one that is always open. Michel would work there as long as he was loaning out the studio. Now that he has gotten it back, the studio is his real workspace, the office having been allotted to day-to-day matters, such as banking or various kinds of mail. Next comes what a stranger would think was a closet signaling the end of the apartment, whereas behind this more or less secret passage is an empty surface of less than a square meter revealing another door opening onto the studio with bathroom and toilet. All the way at the far end of the studio is the bed in which I slept with Thierry and met Gérard, equally isolated by a double door that takes up the entire width of the room. A large balcony follows the length of the picture window and makes a 90-degree angle at the end, running along the entire living room and just until the middle of the studio, which is illuminated at night by the lights of the post-office sorting facility opposite. The single drawback, but only when Michel is there, is that, coming from the studio, it's impossible to knock on the hidden door opening onto the living room to announce yourself since it's padded and produces no noise, therefore risking your being indiscreet. The apartment is big enough to shelter an entire family, and it is obviously not conceived for that—it's the luxury of luxuries.

By a mysterious process with the charm of a fairy tale, it's instantly like being at home for us. For example, it feels completely natural for me to move in with Gérard, Michel not having burdened his offer with any details: just that I stay on rue de Vaugirard as I wish, with whom I wish. The way I see it, I've always lived alone, although my existence at my parents represents the immense majority of my life, because the apartment where I grew up is the archetype of the bourgeois apartment for me, more or less similar to those belonging to the parents of my childhood friends and so different from this one. Moving in with Gérard only seems like a parenthesis in my ontological solitude.

We who are so shy and so unsocial find the apartment perfect for two: there is a place for one in the studio and for the other in Michel's room, located set back at the other end, at the same latitude as the main bathroom and the kitchen, parallel to the beginning of the living room, between the Mahler space and the couch space.

Marc works right next to our apartment, and Hervé lives opposite; I can speak to him from the balcony if I raise my voice and he has the window open. We become loners living in a gang. Because it rapidly seems to us as if we're inhabiting the apartment with a lot more than two—inhabiting signifying so many things—we were already occupants by dint of our acid trips before having had the key. Often, seeing old friends again, I'll hear them exclaim emotionally, "Oh, the rue de Vaugirard!," as if they as well are reminded of the most capital moments of their life, although I've more or less forgotten what the circumstances were.

Marc passes by to say hello as soon as he has a free moment. One Saturday after lunch, he arrives accompanied by a lover, and she suggests taking us to a swimming pool located on the roof of a building three streets away to which she has access because a friend of hers lives there. It's hot, and we readily accept. It is one of those little events that perpetually occur since we've moved in here. In this environment, even I, for whom such a visit to the home of people I don't know would normally be an adventure, can sense that infernal caution I usually feel fading away. Living in this apartment would have no meaning if I refused its effects.

We're alone around the pool except for a bored teenager who speaks to us. It's an English boy of fifteen who's spending his vacation here because his parents exchanged apartments, but he speaks not a word of French and knows no one in Paris. He's very nice, immediately seems to like us a lot and, sympathetic to a situation that reminds us of our own teen years, we suggest he go and have a drink with us. He accepts enthusiastically. Obviously he needs his parents' permission. All five of us get down to that task, taking advantage of the fact that Marc is with his girlfriend. To us a girl seems reassuring for parents, whereas three young men alone could cause worry. They don't show the slightest reticence. Because we've always been stuck in the apartment, we actually don't have a neighborhood café, so we simply bring Anthony back to our place.

The apartment staggers him straightaway. He too must sense something of Michel floating in the air—if the apartment were similar in every way, it still wouldn't be the same if it weren't his, and we all understand that the space itself isn't enough to furnish its exceptional character. Anthony leaves after a reasonable amount of time, suggesting that we come and get him tomorrow if we don't mind.

Which we do, as well as the day after, each time arriving in a four-person delegation composed of three boys and a different girlfriend of Marc. We still see more of an advantage in a girl being with us than in the inconvenience coming from her never being the same one. The parents express so little distrust and give up their son to us in such a casual way that we're happy it's turning out so well for the teenager and that it conforms with the amusement of the situation, as if everything having to do with the apartment on the rue Vaugirard necessarily ends up with a seal of natural fluency. The third evening, when leaving, Anthony, always polite, asks us if he can come tomorrow. "Of course." He says there's no need to pick him up.

From then on, he comes every day. With the exception that he doesn't sleep there, he is living in the apartment like us. We regret not knowing boys his age to introduce to him. Making this vacation the most pleasant possible for the teenager becomes our mission.

We live our life exactly as we wish without his keeping us from anything and attempt only to make him a part of it. We continue to take acid, and that is included in our communal adventure with Anthony. Naturally, we don't offer any to him. We swallow it on the sly when he arrives too early for us to have been able to do that before. But the playful aspect of the LSD, now that experience has helped us master it correctly, deepens our complicity with him. Age is no longer an obstacle, a phenomenon we have already experienced in the opposite sense with Michel. The living room is large enough to inspire the idea of playing Frisbee inside it, as if it were mandatory to take advantage of everything. Our games are epic, enthusiastic, during which laughter prevents our skill from being what it ought to be. When you're bent double and holding your sides, you miss the easiest throws, especially since missing adds to the hilarity while Anthony is reacting in wonder. Moreover, we keep worrying about the projectile striking the Picabia painting hanging in the Mahler corner and that we are therefore protecting like a sort of Fort Alamo, blending the game of daring with that of skill, a combination of Pick-Up Sticks and a western. We're twenty-five years old, and suddenly there's the feeling of seeming like adults who aren't accustomed to it. Certainly Marc isn't around as much because of his job, but for Gérard, who survives from work under the table and has none at the moment, and for me, whose summer hours are very free, the only occupation in existence seems to be spending our time in a magnificent apartment while playing it doesn't matter what game. Anthony still doesn't know that this is accompanied by feedings of LSD. If this teenager weren't there, no one would even notice that our life is taking such a choice turn.

Anthony comes earlier and earlier, stays later and later, sometimes dines with us in the apartment, helps us with our chore, which is watering the plants on the balcony after the setting of the summer sun. The plants don't look like they're doing well, besides, but it isn't as if horticulture were our specialty.

Little by little he talks to us about girls. He's doubtlessly more intuitive than his parents and judges it wiser to do so. Besides, he acts more at ease with Gérard and Marc when it's a matter of horseplay and other masculine games. With me, he's more reserved, as if getting wind of my possible desire. He admits to us that he's still a virgin in a tone that inspires us to want to change that state of affairs. We think of Valérie, familiar as all three of us are with her charms and lack of constraint. I haven't called her for years but do it to offer her the opportunity, and she turns it down, which shocks me since this teenager is so attractive and so willing. (I can imagine myself overcoming my horrible timidity and jumping on that chance if Anthony had presented it to me, but clearly, it's only a girl he wants.) The way the offer was made does justify refusing it, even if it is the kind you just don't say no to. It amuses me to take on the challenge, and I'm laughing until Gérard points out to me the crudeness of such exaggerated enthusiasm in Anthony's presence. I remember the evening when I'd known Valérie for a few months and her sister had spoken with me intimately and easily, which is obviously a family talent. She told the story of an adolescent lover who absolutely wanted to have sex with her. "I wasn't into it. And day after day he would insist, and at the same time I frankly had nothing against it, so that one evening I gave in to make him happy. But what I hadn't understood was that from then on I had no more reason to refuse. It lasted for months. At the end of it, I had to get mad at him, whereas I liked him a lot," she had concluded laughingly; and I admired her tone in speaking about physical love, which no one is obliged to overdo. I obviously have trouble adopting it myself.

Gérard comes up with the idea of the screenings. I myself would never have dared, but I adore his ability to take advantage of fun things; it's the best way to deserve them. In my capacity as a critic I always see films in preview; and because during this season theaters are often three-quarters empty, I have less reservations about asking publicists if I can openly bring others along. Consequently, we all go as a gang. And for the first time in his life Anthony can get into one of those private screening rooms, see the original version of some American films not yet released in Europe, combine the advantage of the showing of a particular film with hearing his own language in another country. Since we speak to him in English and he sees only his parents and us, he isn't making the slightest progress in French. We invite him to dinner at the restaurant after the film, and he seems really happy. We're glad his vacation, which began on a somber note, has turned out a success. What Michel obviously wants is for the apartment on the rue de Vaugirard to benefit the greatest number.

One Sunday, Anthony arrives in the morning at eight-thirty. He's well received and, true to form, is still there at noon, when Gérard and I leave to lunch at our parents'. We don't know what to do, what to say to him. We don't dare put him out, so we leave him alone in the apartment. When we come back almost at the same time, a bit worried, he's finishing the dishes that were still in the sink and the rest of the apartment has been wiped down with a huge cleaning. We don't know what to say to him, and all we need say is thank you.

As content as we are, we view the end of August without apprehension. The charm of the apartment also comes from its being temporary, an address for vacation activities that we had always known would come to an end. We aren't even certain any more of the exact date Michel is returning. "In any case, he's not so stupid that he'd return on August 31 without being forced to," says Gérard, making me laugh at our mock transgression of an implicit taboo. Michel's beyond-normal intelligence is so obvious that, although we don't know exactly how, it's involved at the same time in the pleasure of his friendship and the splendor of his apartment. Moreover, he's certainly not coming back on September 1, either, not being tied to prescribed dates that regulate so many vacations—probably on the 2nd or 3rd, we seem to remember. We decide to hold a farewell party at the apartment on August 31, inviting all those who visited it during the summer; and we will have more than enough time on September 1 in the morning to wash and arrange everything and then clear out well in advance. Anthony is the first invited to that last party.

Everyone is interested in him because his age clashes with the gathering; they're surprised at his presence and still more after he explains it. No one has parents like that. Marc, Gérard and I have never questioned him about it, fearing that it might actually be their indifference that is awarding him such freedom. Anthony doesn't talk about it. We have bought loads of cold stuff to nibble on while being sprawled in the most comfortable places. Suddenly the door opens: Michel. It was in fact August 31 that he'd said he'd return, and he hadn't been worried about being caught in traffic. By the time we've kissed him, he has recovered from his surprise and we from our embarrassment, and he sits on the couch without anyone yet having any idea what the evening will become. He is highly complimented on the apartment. Suddenly—it must be ten o'clock—someone is ringing again. It's Corinne, Valérie's sister. She isn't doing well these days and has been told to come when she wished. She's very surprised by the crowd and the fact that Michel is part of it; as for him, he's tickled by that additional arrival. It's as if somebody were trying to remake the famous gag about the overcrowded cabin from the Marx Brothers, despite the dimensions of the apartment, which would necessitate an enormous number of extras to make the scene effective. "I'm going to sleep at Daniel's," says Michel, cheerfully abandoning us.

On September 1, I dine again on rue de Vaugirard, alone with Michel. We got up at daybreak with Gérard, but without any help from Anthony this time, to do several loads of sheets, washing, drying and vacuum cleaning to make the apartment impeccable. Then we left early enough so that Michel wouldn't have to encounter us again before finally being able to be alone at his place. He phoned that afternoon to see me in the evening, and here I am. I ring, not using my key. Things are back to normal. Michel greets me with his little laugh that seems to be a smile so wide that it requires even more to be expressed, and the look on my face must hardly be any different. Seeing Michel, being assured of his presence, always makes me happy.

It explains why the entrance to that apartment feels like so much fun for me. It's a curious oblong room that is four by twelve feet, not very well lit, with an almost invisible coatrack at its farthest end. What makes it mysterious is quite probably because to leave it and get into the living room, you must first go through a door of unusual dimensions, and all the more so for an entrance. From the living room, when it opens or closes, since it extends to the ceiling and is ten to thirteen feet wide, you'd say it was a section of a moveable wall.

It turns out that the plants, despite our conscientious care—even if it was three in the morning and we were completely stoned, we never forgot to water them—are dead. The tone Michel uses to inform me exonerates me from all responsibility. What interests him is Anthony, and who he was. I tell him the story, which interests him intensely, as if that were exactly his reason for lending us the apartment, and too bad for the plants. "I immediately sensed that he wasn't happy to see me," he says at the end, signifying that Anthony interpreted his return as his own exclusion from the apartment (but at any rate, his parents are taking him back to England very soon). He must also understand how glad I am to see the legitimate owner again, despite the fact that it's making me move out.

2

In winter Michel is invited to teach some courses in the United States, so we move back into the apartment as if nothing had happened. There's even an extra perk: the season and our former caregiving exempt us from our not very earnest concern about the plants on the balcony.

One afternoon, I have a first meeting with a boy younger than me with whom I've been corresponding for years. He wants to be a writer, and his letters have given me an image of him that's a tiny bit Rimbaudian, as he ceaselessly moves from one more or less exotic country to another, snagging various gigs to make a living such as waiter in a café. Seeing him in the flesh and the stories he tells sustain my liking and my attraction. I suggest he come by the apartment that evening for a drink, and he does. Not only do I like him but my attraction for him is becoming more and more obvious. The boy drinks a lot, which jibes with his profile as a young literary adventurer. As for Gérard and I, we're exceptionally sober tonight, not having popped any hallucinogen or opiate. We talk a lot and, since it's already quite late, I signal to the boy that he can stay here to sleep. At first Pierre-Jean is worried that it might cause a problem with Gérard, but he has misjudged our relationship; and Gérard disappears by the living room closet to get to the bed in the studio as a sign of his full and entire approval, so Pierre-Jean accepts without misgivings.

He half undresses, and I get involved with the other half. We lie down naked. Although I never drink, I rapidly feel high from nothing but inhaling his breath as we're kissing. Not as much as he, who's falling asleep as I'm struggling to do my best on his body. Sleep seems to be the greatest pleasure Pierre-Jean can manage in his drunkenness. I'm caught short. My desire hasn't been accepted, nor has it been turned down; and this is a good night even so. In the morning our desire to see each other again is clearly mutual, without either of us knowing when, as Pierre-Jean leaves the apartment, then Paris and France for London.

In the afternoon, Gérard and I go to the screening of an ethnographic documentary that I'm supposed to review. After the opium, morphine is becoming impossible to get; but we've discovered heroin. We take some before going to the movie, and it's my first time. The screening room is almost empty—this film, lasting more than three hours, is intended for a limited audience. We've sunk down into seats as soft as beds, and after a slight time lag I'm sensing the joy of being in love. I have trouble keeping my eyes open; but the film, from what I can see of it, completely matches my state. I find it fascinating and create an enthusiastic account that provokes Gérard's derision—how can I recommend a film that I wasn't able to follow attentively—and swallow it as true in every way? It has to be talented work to provide such an effective accompaniment to my feelings and me. Like morphine, heroin certainly doesn't taste like opium, but there's a softness to it. Returning to normal as the effects dissipate, I anguish a little at not being able to join my lover, who still has no address in England.

There's a wrapped package, candies or little cakes, on the low table in the living room. "What if we ate them?" says Gérard.

Naturally, I burst out that such an act would violate my idea of politeness. "Michel has left for too long a time, they'll be stale," he insists, and I give in. They are cookies, and they are excellent, even if a shred of bad conscience spoils the flavor for me. Hervé stops by in the evening so we can go out to dinner, and I laughingly offer him some, making a reference to a book for adolescents I read when I was one in which a trio of wild kids offer their private tutor part of the cake they're supposed to bring home but then finish devouring on their own—so that during dessert, when their parents express surprise at its absence, they say they've eaten the cake "with monsieur l'abbé," who can't contradict them. Compromising Hervé, who is only too pleased to be, seems like a good policy. The cookies don't last the evening.

The next day I'm preoccupied with another issue. Something itches more and more. I go to a doctor who diagnoses it beyond a doubt as scabies. I'm furious. I've already had them, and they're hell to get rid of. The time before, I'd gone to take a bath treatment for scabies at hôpital Saint-Louis where you ended up with ten or so naked men and boys in a large basin in front of a nurse, who remained very professional in the face of such a spectacle, which actually wasn't very erotic even for me. She painted our skin yellow with a roller, one effect of which was burning the most sensitive parts of the body that nudity allows to be easily reached. I have no desire to go through that again, and I buy the product in the pharmacy to apply it myself, naked on the living room rug, where I dance from one foot to the other trying to resist as best I can the burning sensation.

The next day, when Gérard returns from where I don't know, I announce to him what's going on and tell him that he as well must splash on the product. "But isn't it necessary to do the treatment at the same time in order for it to work?" he says. I'd forgotten, but that's the way it should have been done. Both of us strip. I begin applying it again and this time don't have to wait for the effect. The product is too strong. Two applications in twenty-four hours immediately produce significant irritation.

What is more, the anti-scabies battle has its procedures and protocols for everything. You have to wash your sheets at high temperature, then rewash them, spread DDT everywhere—it's the first time the size of the apartment looks like a drawback to us. The only advantage is that instead of pestering Gérard about my love for Pierre-Jean, I can disguise my amorous anxiety in sanitary precautions. Since the boy is without any possible doubt the contaminator, he'd have to be avoided anyway. It itches, and the first consequence of the irritation is that I mustn't scratch myself. I'm so hopeless when it comes to daily life that I didn't dare start the washing machine before Gérard was there, as if his help were indispensable to me even for that. But he has a meeting, and he has to go out again. "I'm sure you'll figure it out," he says to me as he leaves.

I try. The washing machine is in the kitchen, and until now I've never been the one who uses it. I don't have one at home but do believe myself capable of mastering a device whose use isn't limited to specialists. I turn the temperature dial to maximum, as is necessary, and the dial stays in my hand. I'm completely alone in the apartment, far from my new lover, naked from head to toe, covered with a hideous lotion, burning, itching—losing a little of my nerve. I find the Help number for Brandt washing machines in the phonebook, call it, am transferred from department to department; and they end up telling me I need to go and buy the broken part for 98 centimes in their factory in a remote part of the suburbs. This small cost in relation to the immense inconvenience adds a shabby element to my despair. Even so, I go to gare Saint-Lazare. I don't take the wrong train, or the wrong bus outside the station, the offices aren't closed when I arrive and they have some dials in stock. I come back to the rue de Vaugirard mission accomplished and recount my day to Gérard, who has already gotten back. I'm hoping to give him a guilty conscience for having left me to figure out the machine all alone, as if he'd abandoned me in the middle of the jungle; but his only reaction is laughter, which is also fine with me. His sole penitence is to place the new dial on and turn it himself, just to make sure.

The building entrance doorbell rings, although we're not expecting anyone. It's Daniel, Michel's boyfriend, who didn't go with him to the United States, and he can't do otherwise than notice how the apartment is covered with DDT, a white powder that augurs ill. Nonetheless, he says not a word, excusing himself for disturbing us, which doesn't prevent him from doing just that. "I just came to get the diet cookies Michel prepared for me," he says.

Rue de Vaugirard is a blessing and a curse. There is no one in the world toward whom we want to behave more impeccably than Michel. It's the logical expression of so much affection and respect, and, inevitably, once again, we find ourselves acting like bungling idiots. I—who was so hampered by cookie scruples— have the unpleasant duty of explaining the situation to Daniel; but I buckle down to it and he speaks not a single word of reproach at the end of my paltry account. He leaves without his cookies. Alone in the apartment, we laugh with shame.

In speaking to me about friends in common whose fathers won a Nobel Prize, my brother asks me to what degree people who approach them aren't trying to get to their father. What obviously interests my brother, I know, is the fact that such a question can be asked about us, relatively speaking. I'd never thought of it before. Anyone wanting me for a friend seems so extraordinary that I've never had the idea of searching beyond that and poking around for the motive. Literature excites me, so who knows if I don't excite those in the same position because of my connection to a literary family? I met Pierre-Jean by letter through his texts that I published in the review I'm in charge of. His correspondence quickly warmed, opening the way to what happened next. It matters little what he likes about me as long as he does like me. Just before he left Paris, I found out a position in the stockroom was opening up at Les éditions de Minuit, and I told him I could intercede to get him the job, which wouldn't be any worse than being a waiter in a café. He'd also be in Paris—a motivation, incidentally, that is more mine than his. We'll contact each other again, then, about this too. But no news has come, and I'm suffering obsessively. I fall upon *A Lover's Discourse: Fragments* (*Fragments d'un discours amoureux*) in the living room library, one of the rare books by Barthes I haven't read, and I gorge myself on it. I leaf through it ceaselessly, mini-chapter by mini-chapter: everything is there.

Several weeks after my lover has disappeared, as I'm despairingly thinking about still having no news, I stop by my place with Marc to pick up some clean things and get my mail. It could be that Pierre-Jean hadn't noted the address where we slept together. Bingo. I have a postcard, coming not from London but from Sydney, no guarantee of meeting very soon and ending with the words "I love you." Joyously I show it to Marc as proof, crow about it, before returning more cheerfully to rue de Vaugirard.

Love is excellent as a feeling, but it's not bad as a practice either, something I lack. I'm starting a correspondence with Pierre-Jean that's too deprived of action for my taste. Love has a different appeal when you see each other and everything that entails. Once again I fall back on *A Lover's Discourse*.

I don't see Pierre-Jean again before Michel returns. I discuss it with Michel as soon as possible, and he listens attentively with no sign of boredom, which those in love pick up on with great sensitivity. I speak to him about it again at the next dinner, then regularly on the telephone. Pierre-Jean is coming back to France but not to Paris. Seeing each other is complicated, and conflict is in the air. I don't know what to do. I ask Michel's advice about anything at all, and he gives it willingly, never presenting it as absolutely indispensable. He doesn't believe that such advice is necessarily good. He merely unburdens me of the responsibility for having acted one way or another on my own initiative. I trust him enough to accept the consequences of my conduct as unavoidable and not as the result of some idiotic strategy. Such effectiveness is an absolutely integral part of his advice. When it comes to the rest, Michel is simply not in control of the situation.

The truth is that I'm leaving the matter in his hands without realizing it. Never would I have imagined experiencing such intimacy with a man his age, all the less so with him. I'm so devoted to Michel that I have no trouble supposing he feels the same way. Everything about his behavior shows it. It's not something to suppose but something that has been interiorized without having thought about it.

In speaking about other things, Michel informs me later in passing that the washing machine caused an unexplainable flood at the downstairs neighbors' during my stay.

3

The story with Pierre-Jean runs afoul, leaving me alcohol as its first-class legacy. The drunkenness pulled from his breath that first evening educated me. In the bar where I hang out with Hervé, in order to find the courage to transform my desire into enjoyment and tackle anyone whose beauty makes him an inaccessible being, I now drink a gin and tonic or two, not counting those to which the unfolding of the rest of the evening leads. One evening, after Hervé has tactfully left me alone there, I take on a boy who pleases me terribly. I can easily see that he hasn't decided at first, but I have confidence in my conversational skills and actually do take him home to my place at the very end of the evening. Strange night. I have the sensation of being in love with him and the premonition I'll never see him again. After the sex, I purposely keep from sleeping so that I can fill up on his presence and his nakedness. In the morning he leaves no telephone number. I don't succeed in seeing him again, and it breaks my heart.

Whereas I drove Michel mad with Pierre-Jean, it becomes tooth and nail with Valentin, who at least has the advantage of creating a more cheerful environment for the relationship than Pierre-Jean could. "Yes, let's call him more playful," an amused Michel answers when I decide it's a good idea to explain the difference between my old and my new loves to him. It makes more sense in terms of Valentin, but that story isn't too glorious either. "After all, you've never seen him in the light of day," Hervé says to me when I regale him with the boy's beauty, because I'd met Valentin after night had fallen, he left my apartment early in the morning and hasn't provided me with another chance to set eyes on him. He calls sometimes and doesn't say when he'll call back, so that I'm always afraid of missing his call by leaving the house.

I dine alone with Michel on rue de Vaugirard the evening of my birthday. That is at least what was planned. However, bit by bit, Gérard, Hervé, Marc, Didier and Hélie come out from behind the chairs, couch and false closet leading to the studio. Hélie is a childhood friend who has been out of touch since mid adolescence and who has reappeared. Didier is a new friend whom I helped meet Michel. A surprise is so rare in my family tradition that this is a complete one. I'm touched, of course, but it isn't what I was expecting even in the domain of the unexpected. "It's Valentin I would have been thrilled to see," I say to Gérard, who reacts as if he were taking full responsibility for the failure of not having been able to bring him and answers, "I know. Something I would have really liked."

Between the moment when Michel announces that he's going to travel—which is currently his discreet way of lending the apartment as if it would be an aberration to leave it unoccupied for a single day—and the instant when we move in, Valentin hasn't called. As a result, I haven't been able to give him the number where I can be reached from now on. Therefore, the rue de Vaugirard move—from now on the generic name embodying the apartment and its way of life—is a little less joyous than usual, but joyous nevertheless. By chance, Valentin calls on a day when I go by my place to pick up some possessions, and three days later he calls rue de Vaugirard, something he starts doing regularly.

The endless calls usually come when I'm alone in the sun-filled, bright apartment, which is too big for me, calls that I prolong as much as I can without seeming too much as if I'm doing it, taking advantage of the infinitely long cord to walk up and down the living room or sitting cross-legged on the carpet. One evening, Valentin makes a date to meet in a subway station. At the agreed-upon hour he isn't there, nor is he there an hour later when I finally give up waiting for him, a decision that tears me apart. I come back to rue de Vaugirard to recount my misfortune to Gérard, but no one can do anything about it. Valentin stops calling.

One morning, I get out of Michel's bed with the dream I had that night still in my head. Its narrative is as simple as its meaning: I was making love with Valentin. Waking up is harsh. I'm as empty as a landscape. Something in my life is forever escaping me. Never have I so concretely seen how unobtainable happiness is. Gérard tells me to get over Valentin, voicing it so gently that it demonstrates his assurance that it's the solution—and that I'd be blatantly flaunting my weakness by not submitting to it. So I try to forget. At a party I cruise everyone I meet, a boy with whom it doesn't work, another boy with whom it doesn't work, a girl with whom it works. I bring her back to rue de Vaugirard. Short night. It's been years since I spent the night with a girl, and this is no girl who'll save me from Valentin; nor will any girl nor person other than him.

The last girl with whom I slept before this one goes back several years. She was then a former lover, having returned to my studio with the intention of staying the night; and she'd spoken to me about her lover, repeating what this guy said about me in one terse sentence crammed with reproaches: I was a fag, a druggie and a friend of Michel Foucault. I'd repeated those words to Hervé, not daring to tell Michel, but Hervé took on the mission of transmitting it straight off and Michel had been thrilled, never having suspected that all by himself he could be a vice as much of a household word as drugs and homosexuality. As for me, I took advantage of it to have something to hold against the boy: because it was as if I was coming from the right and had the right of way—it would be a shame not to get angry with somebody when it was completely your right to do it. Nevertheless, I can't manage having a falling out with Valentin, even though it would obviously be the best thing to do. It would not only be reasonable but a way to keep from losing my reason.

After Pierre-Jean, Valentin: I'm in love living in the apartment, which is becoming the spatial version of my elation and my wish to squelch it. *A Lover's Discourse*, again. I never read it at home, always on rue de Vaugirard. I'm right smack in the middle of what Barthes calls the "*non-vouloir-saisir*," the need to renounce my lover for good, so that it wouldn't be a strategy of indifference but a shattering and lusterless reality. I can't do it. For me that's what it is, that orgasm in the negative that has to be called the little death, when it's necessary to push a part of yourself to commit suicide.

I know that I'm still young, but I'm nostalgic for youth. I see it as an opportunity, a unique chance. I mustn't fail myself.

You could also call this a café, a house of assignation: all our friends stop by when we're living at rue de Vaugirard and they are in the neighborhood. It's the place we always meet before going to dinner. It's where we encounter Richard, the boy living with Didier, who learns that Gérard has an urgent need of money and offers him a three-month contract at Europe Assistance where he himself has a more or less important position. Despite his dread of bosses, given the situation, Gérard accepts. At the job, the temps recruited by Richard before clearly show he is part of a particular kind of network, and everyone assumes that Richard is gay. He fears this could be a hindrance to the relationship he'd like to pursue with a girl, but it isn't at all. On the contrary,

Véronique quickly becomes intimate with such an appealing boy that no gross sexual appetite has attracted to her, which leads to her becoming delighted at being undeceived one day to discover a sexual appetite that's reciprocal, gross and refined and satisfied day after day. They move in together, so when Gérard and I take over (we're beginning to adopt that tone as part of the game) the rue de Vaugirard, she comes too.

As for me, I've just spent the night with a new boy—Patrick— whom I invite to come over for another. He accepts, one thing leads to another and he moves into rue de Vaugirard too. Now there are two couples living here, which changes nothing but for the better. I haven't given Patrick a key. I just met him in a bar, know almost nothing about him and this is Michel's apartment. Gérard gives him one, doubtlessly out of thoughtfulness for me. The boy is twenty, lives in the suburbs at his mother's with his cat. I still have Valentin under my skin, find this new boy appealing, but I'm not in love with him. Patrick asks to bring his pet to the house. We don't care if he does and aren't aware that Michel is allergic to it, so we accept. Since they have taken to each other and Véronique has a car, in the evening she goes with Patrick to get the cat. Gérard and I are alone in the place. We have fun imagining that Véronique and Patrick have actually conned us with that scenario and simply wanted to take off together. We'll never set eyes on them again. Gérard even adds a detail about their not feeling guilty about it, figuring that the two of us have such an excellent rapport that we'll be lucky to end up alone together in the apartment and will still be happy. It's false, it's true, it's all funny; or, in any case, makes us laugh.

We perfect our humor. One afternoon, we take acid with Marc, just the three of us. We're comfortably sitting not too far from one another but in different corners. Marc is talking about the blue sweater I'm wearing and that he thinks is an attractive shade, and it's getting darker and darker, he remarks, under the effect of the hallucinations. "It's very pretty darker, you can go for it," says Marc jokingly, and it is a joke but one that pleases us especially because of its effective mix of realities, taking into account that what he sees is the effect of the drug (but he's seeing it even so), and as if, while the seconds flowed by, the color of the sweater were uniquely the product of its possessor's will—my own—as if I were controlling actual light and dark from deep inside my brain. We're happy to have mastered acid to the extent of being able to make jokes having to do with it, jokes that would have no meaning in another frame of mind but still arise from humor and not only from convulsive giggling.

Wacky faces on acid please us the most—the ability to condense in a single expression or unique gesture or appropriate tone for a simple word an entire account and its moral indications that the others can grasp perfectly in the space of an instant. The swiftness of this has comic profundity, and never has the imagination been so well rewarded. One evening, Marc takes Gérard and me to a friend's party. Very quickly we become bored. Moreover, there aren't enough seats, and we're tired of standing up. Gérard unearths an unoccupied chair in the room adjoining the living room, where the party isn't going full blast, and sits down there relieved. I go with him. Spontaneously, a game takes shape consisting in getting the seated person out of his chair and putting yourself in his place. The only weapon that we allow ourselves in order to make this happen is a sentence expressing a complete fiction that won't allow any way out for the seated person whose politeness and honesty has to force him to stand up: "You're wanted on the telephone," "M. Martin is waiting for you in his office," "Your wife and child are doing well, you must be impatient to see them." And that lasts an insane amount of time, as we spout sentences that are more and more outrageous, polished, and spend our time sitting and standing, no longer tired but excited, and finally realize that the living room is now deserted and that all the guests are in the little room that has become the highlight of the party, the place where people are having fun. And we have the feeling not only of being able to call upon acid even when we're not on it, as if our imaginations had acquired the power to take permanent advantage of the freedom that is sometimes chemically granted us, but of now possessing the gift of bringing the rue de Vaugirard with us and exporting it anywhere at all.

This is our day-to-day reality, even if we are conscious of how extraordinary it is, and that is why we take advantage of it as if the apartment were its own drug all by itself. Even so, when it comes to LSD, the norm is to take it there with Michel. There are three of us in the studio (Marc is spending the weekend at some arts festival or other, but with a girlfriend), which we've moved into to watch films. The amateurism of our early sessions is over. All the devices have been put in working order beforehand. We chose a Marx Brothers again, not because we have a taste for repetition but, as is the case with Mahler, because we sense that regardless of our enjoyment, everything is connected only by a thread that must be handled carefully. It's their last film, *Love Happy*, and actually dates long after the previous. A slight uneasiness immediately materializes. There is nothing to say against *Love Happy* aside from the fact that the brothers are old, too old to seem funny. In the state in which we are, you may be ready to laugh at anything, but we don't laugh at this film. The gags don't reach us, and we see nothing other than the Marx Brothers' wrinkles, fatigue. The film has a strong emotional effect on us. It obviously would have been more suitable for coming down from acid than when the drug is in full force, apart from the fact that this film needs acid to be deconstructed under our eyes. We were there to laugh, and here we are being moved.

There has been a misunderstanding. We're afraid of the feelings we're having. Frankly speaking, it's not as if we're plunging into a bad trip; we're only that much closer to overstepping the line. This isn't the first time we've had an experience like this since we've been taking acid together. Each of us has always had some difficult moments to manage in the course of the afternoon, but it's the first time we're doing it all together—although we resist, hold on, and a little minus changes slightly into a little plus. Even so, it didn't go wrong by much.

Michael's age is something to think about. We admire his ability to take LSD at a ripe age, because each dose carries a kind of radical putting into question that youth, we think, is more likely to bear, and we admire his courage. We have the feeling that binging on LSD is a sign of health, and so many people don't dare. Sometimes, during the trip, I have an extraordinary compassion for my father whom I love, whose intelligence and happiness I think acid would enhance, and who I know would never even imagine taking it of his own free will. For me that is one of the characteristics of acid that moves me in a disproportionate way when I'm under its effect, feeling so grievously, as if in active support of the rest of humanity, the misfortunes created only by conventions, the joys you consider it essential to deprive yourself of.

As usual, once we've come down from the LSD, Michel heats something up for us. Acid takes so much out of you, and you have to put yourself together again. The three of us eat at the kitchen table. Michel moves his fork very rapidly. I have the impression that I'm doing the same, but Gérard later tells me when we're alone, "It's crazy how Michel always seems so young but seems so old when he eats." He's never the one with a nasty word, so I'm convinced. I wonder if I seem old too. I sense an unpleasant old age in me that keeps me in check more than it settles me down.

4

Hélie is a friend from childhood. He's almost part of the family. He knows my parents, and I know his. He uses the informal "you" with my father and has already spent vacations at my grandparents', as I have with his family. We fell out of touch while we were teenagers, when he went to another high school, abandoning the one where we knew each other and where I was pulling a fast one, getting better grades by making most of the teachers think I was nicer. I remember one summer, my annoyed cousin said to him about me, "But why are you always imitating him?", and that statement made an impression on me, less than it must have on him. The idea of being a model for anything at all had never entered my mind.

Since we've become young men I like introducing him to my friends, now that I have some. They are the best part of me I have to offer. Anyone who got to know me only through them would have a fantastic idea of me. No matter how much of my adolescence I spent reading, Hélie is still much more cultured than I am in every aspect. Apparently, not only did he meet human beings during the period when we weren't in touch, he also read most of what I did, and spy or science fiction novels by the hundreds, too. He loves classical music as much as he does French variety (my specialty), not to mention rock or jazz. When it comes to painting, he has the same familial familiarity with it as I do with literature. As a young man, he still possesses the sane intelligence, kindness and sensitivity that appealed to me as a child.

He takes a sudden dislike of Marc, for a reason that escapes us but has to do with the fact that Bella, the girl with whom Marc spent the first acid trip in New York and had a love affair, has been Hélie's friend for years (their families were close). Obviously, he judges her worthy of a better match. The truth is that Marc's affectionate brutality can sometimes be exasperating—when he kisses you to say hello or goodbye his embrace and his lips give the impression that he's going to crush your teeth or bones. He's ostentatious, as if he were a Jewish mother despite the fact that there's no genetic reason to justify having to put up with it. But his excessive benevolence is real, and he's a fantastic companion. Hélie quickly becomes friends with Gérard. Michel also appreciates him, and he becomes familiar with the rue Vaugirard.

We introduce him to acid, he who deepens everything that he touches. Aside from his immense literary and artistic knowledge, he has studied mathematics, brilliantly passing the most select competitive exams, as a result of which he became a math teacher, having just left his post in Reims, which was making life complicated, to find work in a private Parisian school. To our eyes, despite his successes, he's the one who has the least exciting life of all of us. It's as if he were misdirected, and sometimes he makes us feel self-conscious. "He's so squeamish that you're always afraid of being vulgar when you get close to him," Bella will tell me. It's something to which I'm all the more sensitive because my own overly long adolescence, whether through refinement or simple panic, made me fear the same thing until I met Valérie, Marc, Thierry, Gérard, Michel and Hervé.

One evening on acid at rue de Vaugirard, we suddenly decide to go out and take the subway. We're still stoned, more than we think. The subway car is almost empty. However, Véronique is sitting opposite a lady and Gérard and I on the bench next to them. We play at speaking to Véronique as if we don't know her and cruise her like punks with a vocabulary that isn't ours. She responds with irritation, just as the implicit rules of the situation demand. This lasts for several stations. When we get off, Hélie lectures Gérard and me. We should have been more careful, because the woman sitting opposite Véronique was terrified and took it all seriously. We're flabbergasted that he hadn't told us earlier, when we hadn't understood the disagreeable aspect of the situation. Now it serves nothing. In the audit of the moral sense caused by acid, Hélie remains theoretician of the absolute when, with indeterminate success, we were only aspiring to a relative practical experience.

For a five-person acid trip that includes Michel and Marc, Hélie arrives on rue de Vaugirard with his records. He is fussy, so attached to them that he's cautious about using them. Only generosity has made him take them out of his home. Once already, when it was just the three of us, instead of Mahler, Marc had had us listen to Marc-Antoine Charpentier, whom he adores, and it hadn't been convincing. The music wasn't suitable, and we had put a stop to it before becoming totally bored to death. In this case, Hélie has brought *La Périchole* so boredom isn't the most likely, especially since I adore Offenbach who has the power to put me in a cheerful mood. But comic opera falls short of taking charge of the meditative aspect of the LSD. Even its virtuosity seems coarse and doesn't work. All of us control our expression before demanding a program change for the second record to be played, which greatly surprises Hélie, who hadn't noticed there was any problem. We need the support of Michel, a well-informed music lover who's beyond suspicion, to make Hélie give in without ascribing this musical incompatibility to our ineptitude.

On December 31, Michel is invited to a New Year's Eve party and suggests we take LSD at rue de Vaugirard where he'll join us not too late, even before the stroke of New Year's. All four of us come over, with Hélie and Marc. We hang out and eat until midnight. We're impatient because we have nothing else to do other than the acid. Michel doesn't show up, and at 1AM we take it. Michel only returns much later, when the acid has really come on, and he's going to sleep again at Daniel's, who is with him. Never before have we taken LSD this late, and its effects last the entire night. Maybe it wasn't such a good idea. Not to mention the fact that Hélie, informed as well about film as he is about everything else, has decided to choose a movie after our telling him we often watch them in these circumstances. It's *The Wizard of Oz*. Very quickly Gérard and I are convinced that Hélie chose that work for its own qualities, not because of any relationship to the drug. The film upsets us, watching it is a drag and we abandon it to go sit in another part of the apartment, but we get bored. It's the last thing you'd expect from acid, but that's the word for it—not some horrible freak-out or vague suicidal impulse—just boredom, pure and simple. Both of us leave the apartment to go walk in deserted and icy Paris during the early morning hours of January 1. We stand our ground, more moved by our increasingly obvious closeness than by what has called it into action. Hélie doesn't understand and is still boasting about his film when we come back less messed up than you'd expect.

A few hours later, I'm on the way to lunch at my family's for January 1, feeling drained and disoriented. The phone rings during the meal; my mother answers and announces that it's for me. It has been centuries since anyone called me at my parents. It's Michel, who has found my forgotten wallet and hurried to phone before I become worried. I'd had no idea and will stop by rue de Vaugirard again after lunch. When I arrive there, fatigue, laced with a feeling of sensuality, make me want to lie down. The night of acid has made me lose my bearings. Recounting his meeting during hitchhiking with Thierry who had ended up in his bed, Michel told me one day how Thierry, at the decisive moment, had asked Michel if what he really wanted was to let him go home. And Michel made it clear that it was actually up to Thierry—the younger man—to ask such a question, to take the initiative. On January 1, if Michel wants to have sex with me, it's a deal. There's no way he can't see it, but I don't say a thing, because I'm not particularly keen on it, just ready to. Michel doesn't try anything, or say anything but those words that will put me right again and that he has the gift of choosing. His preferring not to have sex with me pleases me too.

Hélie invites Michel to dinner with us at his place. Since the fiasco organized by Hervé when we first knew each other, no one has risked it. We have the feeling that deep down it makes Michel less embarrassed to have us over than for him to change locations, even when he has nothing to heat up in his kitchen, and that we're luckier to be his friends than he ours, that we're not going to pretend to be his equals, if only in the way we interact. A few days before the dinner, which had been scheduled a long time ago, Hervé finds out he'll be in Munich on that day for a theater festival that his magazine is asking him to cover. He suggests that I go with him, be sent there by my own magazine, as we've managed to do many times when one of us is traveling for professional reasons. Our respective editors are aware of our interests and act to encourage our friendship. While talking to Michel, I tell him we'll both be absent, and he tells me to ask Hélie to postpone the dinner. Hervé and I are the ones he knows best. We're the ones with whom he's most at ease and postponing the dinner is the obvious thing to do. Awkward as it becomes, I have to imply this too much to Hélie, because he holds fast. He refuses to change anything at all. After all,

Michel's the most important guest, and too bad for us if we can't be there. I'm stunned about having to tell Michel about the failure of a mission that both of us believed was of child-like simplicity.

Didier explained to me later that the evening of the dinner, while Hervé and I were partying in Munich, he went to rue de Vaugirard to pick up Michel and that they took a taxi for Hélie's place. They were swallowed up in an immense traffic jam caused by a police demonstration against the minister of justice, and Michel, easily recognizable, found himself surrounded by furious policemen who were obviously not on his side. Hélie and Didier are hardly fond of each other, and Didier added with satisfaction that Michel ended up singing the praises of Hélie's hospitality between clenched teeth in a tone sweetly redolent of annoyance.

The death of Hélie's father destabilizes him. He spends ages at rue de Vaugirard, coming with me when I dine at Michel's and even often arriving in the afternoon, well before the dinner hour to be comforted by Michel. Hélie thinks of it as the normal, tasteful thing to do, making it known that he too would do all he could for Michel. What he doesn't take into consideration is that Michel, if he ever did turn to us in a difficult situation, might have less expectations.

Hélie invites Gérard and me to his mother's country house, about 60 miles from Paris, where I spent many weekends and vacations with him as a child. His father has died ten days ago, and he suggests all three of us take acid, which he has on hand. Given the circumstances, we try to dissuade him, and it comes to naught—in fact, these are precisely the circumstances in which he feels justified. Of course, during the acid trip, he laughs a lot less than us. Gérard and I experience it our way, merely checking regularly that everything is all right. We understand that for him it's an ordeal, that he's using the LSD as a test. This is so different from our use that we feel sorry for him, with that youthful satisfaction in viewing luck as a merit, in feeling gently superior.

From then on, life is stable: when Michel is in Paris, I stay at my place, not counting dinners; when Michel is away, be it only for a few days, Gérard and I hightail it over to rue de Vaugirard, and the whole gang knows about it. And pronto, it's time for acid. On me it has a diuretic effect. Five times per trip, I find myself in the bathroom. It's located in the hallway parallel to the living room, behind the partition of the library and between Michel's bedroom and the kitchen. It's the only room in the apartment that doesn't have a window. The light there is entirely artificial, weak and not very pleasant. For me the bathroom becomes linked to LSD, the sound of my urine hitting the water in the confinement of that minuscule room with its strange lighting. One of Gérard's first pieces of advice, before the first acid trip, was not to look at yourself in the mirror; your own face looking deformed can lead to a bad trip. But the demon of perversity always forces me to raise my eyes to the mirror in the bathroom while washing my hands after pissing, at first fleetingly and then more and more regularly in the course of sessions, studying myself in the glass. My features have a different kind of gauntness with traces of yellow and green, ochre. At first I think I look like Dracula, and this feeling grows into an obvious fact. I accept it without a problem. I am what I am, the spitting image of Dracula without the existence of the original, an inhabitant of this toilet, this apartment.

Michel's fame, his reputation, certainly have their impact on my affection for him. But what kind of affection? I really do love him. One afternoon on acid at rue de Vaugirard, we turn on the television and it announces the death in exile of the Shah. Although he had held it against Michel for having expressed himself as he did about Iran, I feel a spurt of anxiety, in all evidence shared by Gérard, about such news looming up in such uncontrollable circumstances. The fact of anyone at all wishing the slightest harm to Michel seems like an injustice to us, a miscomprehension of what ought to be the laws of the universe. Once again, it feels like a narrow escape, but we correctly handle that intrusive information. Nothing indicates that Michel himself has been struck by it.

One day, Michel doesn't take acid with us. The plan had included five, we four including Marc, plus Alain, a friend of Michel who is about a dozen years older than us and with whom we get along well. We're on rue de Vaugirard at the agreed-upon time. Michel says that he doesn't feel like it, but that this doesn't prevent us from taking advantage of it. He'll shut himself up in the studio where there's less of a chance that we would go since we haven't rented a film this time. Given the situation, Alain also will abstain and will be kind enough to stay and talk with Michel while we are high. But he puts his dose of acid in his pocket to make use of it elsewhere, with other people. That strikes us by eclipsing his generosity in supporting Michel. With our peculiar reasoning, we don't understand in what way taking acid on rue de Vaugirard is anything like doing it outside of the rue de Vaugirard, nor in what way not taking it on the premises authorizes carrying it elsewhere. Later, in front of Michel, I assess I don't know what ill will I feel toward Alain who seems so humble yet isn't so much as that. "We're always surprised that others want the same thing we do," he says to put me in my place.

When Michel's away, acid days happen more often. There are always chance occurrences coming at a bad time and about which we're not too concerned. Daniel phones looking for a key, guides me to some furniture containing the drawer where all of them are kept and asks whether I can see one he needs that looks like this or like that among a welter of them that seems limitless. At that point in the conversation, my helplessness becomes obvious, and I'm forced to admit what I was hiding for some unknown reason—the fact that I'm stoned to the gills on acid and can't for the life of me tell the difference between even two keys. Daniel comes by just to find it himself, taking care not to disturb us.

Now that, according to Gérard's merry expression, Michel has "invaded" the studio—in other words, is no longer loaning it to Thierry, who caused that change himself by traveling around the world—our days on acid when I'm confused about exactly what I'm in control of have become the source of a new fear. Although we don't dare cast the slightest glance on the hundreds and hundreds of pages of manuscript ceaselessly piling up that Hervé will call Michel's infinite book, we're afraid of chucking them out the window (or into a fire organized for the occasion, or down the garbage chute while hoping it won't plug it up, or into a full tub where a nice little bath like the one in New York never does any harm). We talk about it to ward off such a bad fate. We'd prefer throwing ourselves out the window by the balcony as we sometimes discuss happening while peaking on LSD. It's a relief to see the manuscript go through the months, seasons, years, without anything bad happening to it or to us.

We never let the chance to get hold of some acid go by. One evening a friend leaves us two doses, because we resented it when he claimed he wanted to throw them out under the excuse that he'd tried some from the same source without it having the slightest effect. We keep them in reserve for ourselves. You never know, and we'll sleep better with them on hand. In the morning, I have a meeting at noon with Gérard in a big eyewear store to choose a new pair of glasses. When I go to the kitchen for breakfast, Gérard has already gone out but has left a note on the table saying that he has taken the acid to keep it from going stale, especially since it's of bad quality, and that I should do the same. The little piece of blotter paper is lying on the note, and I swallow it by way of breakfast. No effect, as if it were any old piece of paper. We aren't even thinking about it any more when we meet up to choose my frames. It's only at the moment when the clerk puts a pair of glasses on my nose and suggests I check myself out in one of the millions of mirrors in that store that we understand we're stoned to the tits. The last thing you should do at such a moment is look at yourself in a mirror, and mirrors abound on these thousands of square feet—a Dracula orgy. What is more, just as happened with the key, there's no way of making sense of this variety of glasses, all of them more hallucinogenic than the next. We bolt from the store doubled up. This is the first time that LSD has taken us unaware. Another reason, just as well, to feel almost invulnerable. Until now, we've taken each dose of acid with a thousand precautions. This is the first time we've behaved with such reprehensible offhandedness, and it hasn't led to the slightest disadvantage. On the contrary, being on a trip without expecting it has a special charm.

Certainly there was the one on December 31, which was so-so, but suddenly I'm considering the fantasy of a bad acid trip that would allow me to explore the flip side of pleasure just as scrupulously. Maybe it would be horrible, but it would be a state of mind, an object of study without which I will die like an illiterate. When I talk to him about it, Michel refers me to the fantasy of ruination from a more broad-ranging point of view, the gambler who in one evening has become indebted for life, the drug addict at the mercy of any kind of dealer at all. I'm not the only one with such thoughts.

Drugs: I get to know them. Now I sometimes end up sniffing heroin when I'm not doing acid. However, when I have a gram at my place, I can hold onto it for a month, in other words, sample it at an acceptable frequency without risk. My rule is never to take any of it alone, which obviously limits my use, not to mention that you're less at risk for getting hooked if you also have to bear the costs of buying it for a buddy. After a while, in our thirst for knowledge (isn't education fun?), Gérard and I want to study taking a fix as well. We don't know anything about the alleged immediate flash of sweet brutality brought on by injection. I can't bear shots, but I don't want to be on the wrong side of tolerance, like all those eternal acid virgins. So we get hold of some syringes and try the experience. But we're so scared—not about its effect but about the procedure itself—that I refuse to do it, being too aware of my clumsiness, and offer my arm to Gérard (which also avoids the risk of getting hooked that way, since I'd always need someone else to stick a needle into my vein). We're so anxious about this new experience that we calm down by sniffing a little heroin before injecting it, so that the flash turns out not what it ought to be.

Before I've ever taken cocaine, Hélie offers me some on rue de Vaugirard, and it's worse than the first acid trip. I feel absolutely nothing, don't see any difference between it and my normal state. "Even so, you've been talking without stopping for three quarters of an hour," he said.

All of Hélie's lovers whom I meet are the opposite of him. Their vulgar minds jar with his refinement. Gérard is just as surprised by it as I am, but Hervé and Michel don't believe me when I tell them. Hervé explains to me that it's normal to feel a kind of jealous uneasiness for friends you've known since childhood. It doesn't ring true for me, but that would be difficult to discuss. On an evening in front of the TV at my place, where Michel, contrary to his habits, has stopped by after dinner, Hélie arrives with his lover of the moment and pushes him in our faces. The night is spoiled by the obvious fact that the lover is making a disastrous impression on everybody. "Your embarrassment about Hélie comes from what you see in him that you could have become," Hervé tells me the next day on the phone with turn-coat exaggeration. I like what he says because, as a result of my miraculous encounters, I actually have felt that I've escaped something indefinable, and it could very well be that.

When I come back to rue de Vaugirard after being away for a week, it turns out Hélie slept there the night before. "He wanted to so much," Gérard explains. I don't like it—it rattles me as if he'd taken advantage of the fact of my not being there. All I ask is to share this place with everybody, and I wouldn't like him to spoil it for us. For both Gérard and me there are eight days left before having to go home, and to clarify the atmosphere of happiness on rue de Vaugirard, Gérard dares say, "What if Michel died?", meaning "What if Michel weren't coming back?", thereby abandoning the apartment to us. We're perfectly aware we would have nothing to gain from that, but death isn't the issue, and that's the distinction: nowhere are we more alive than on rue de Vaugirard.

5

Books aren't only what I want out of life; but even so, I can't imagine it without them. They replenish my future. Hervé got to know Michel by sending a text he had just published to his prestigious neighbor. The fact that he wanted to be published in the review I edit was a determining factor of our own encounter. My own desire to write novels is always palpable in my relationship with Michel.

In the middle of my Valentinian period, my father agrees to publish a book by Hervé, which delights him. It's something for me as well. I haven't written a novel yet, although I'm convinced I will; and in my eyes, my father, aside from his merits as a publisher, is enhanced by his paternal status. I discuss this with Michel one evening after dinner in the tranquil Mahler corner. The music we listen to is reserved for LSD, but we've shared so many hours listening to the symphonies "Titan" and "Resurrection" that no place in the apartment seems more intimate. I'm not jealous of Hervé being with another boy, no more than I would be about Valentin having multiple partners, as long as I was one. But I admit to Michel that I am jealous of Hervé for his manuscript—pleased and happy for my friend—but jealous. It feels like a real confession. Michel answers that it's normal to be jealous of your friends, something I interpret in a way that does me the greatest good: you can only be jealous of someone you respect, a realization that lessens the feeling and its perverse effects.

Before meeting Hervé, Hélie read some of his texts in the review I edit. Later, when Hervé is republishing several of those stories in a book, Hélie remarks that they were fine for the review but that, even so, a book is something else. The remark surprises me. Obviously it was prompted by something other than his usual kindness. Michel, who speaks highly of Hélie's generosity, explains to me that he's definitely not jealous of either Hervé or me but of our relationship. I agree that there's something to that.

One day when I'm alone on rue de Vaugirard, I happen upon a book by Hervé in the library and am indiscreet enough to read the dedication. It's written to Michel in an understated way: "To my neighbor," printed on the first page. And yet, when the book came out, Hervé had already moved. Accordingly, on Michel's copy of the book he has crossed out the "To" in order to add six words with a pen that with the remaining printed words reads, "For Michel, who will always be my neighbor." I feel the same way. Michel once told me that it's best to be neighbors rather than live together, which describes his situation with Daniel, whose apartment is only a couple of minutes away. Even when Gérard and I are living together on rue de Vaugirard, I feel like his neighbor. The apartment is big enough for two to be there without disturbing each other, and Michel's announced return supplies a time limit to the experience that preserves it from feeling like eternity, or fate, which characterizes all those who cohabit. I feel like I'm part of a neighborhood gang. My own apartment is at the other end of Paris, but I'm sharing Michel's, even if it's in a peculiar spatiotemporal fashion. Sometimes, without mulling it over, I feel as if there can't be any connection that is stronger. It's not like living together out of habit or sexual predilection; it's a choice that is perpetually renewed, and always new. It's an original invention, a way of life that Michel and I may be the only two in the world to share.

My father is happy, probably proud as well, when he learns of my friendship with Michel, aware as he is of the personal and social advantages that come from frequenting great men. He quickly finds it good to inform me that it's public knowledge that Michel is full of compliments, so exaggerated that he can't believe in them himself. This comes just short of his being a flatterer. I don't see any ill will in it. My father just wants to keep me from falling into a trap more or less initiated by homosexuality, and I need to keep a cool head. My father's restraint sometimes attains the theatrical. It's worth more to err by a weak compliment than an excessive one. That is one concept of justice.

I've had just about enough of those film reviews in which I panned a movie with a few lines and am glad to be writing about books for the newspaper, working in a domain I know better, and only concerning works I like. One day when Michel is speaking to me about a friend in common and expresses annoyance about how closed his mind is, how the boy has a preconceived notion about everything, I answer that I do, too, to which Michel retorts that certainly I also have an opinion about everything but that I change it at the first convincing argument. And this pleases me like an inhabitual compliment. Remaining rigidly faithful to an opinion is behavior that has its enthusiastic partisans, and it's also true that I myself actually enjoy changing my mind. Being confronted with the fugitive nature of even a certainty seems to be exactly what life is about.

Full of joy at every instant, frequently shaken by bursts of hilarity about what I reckon are strokes of inspiration, I write a novel, a kind of rustic epic about despicable acts. Writers often employ the imperfect subjunctive to evoke coarse sexuality, which gives their work the imprimatur of a lofty genre—I'm having fun dealing with low-brow pornography, perversions without much depth rendered in a language not so much spoken as thought. I blend my taste for paradoxical reasoning with the literary practice of prostitution, pedophilia and scatology seen under an angle I think of as original, a horrifying vision of family life. I have Michel and Hervé read the manuscript. Hervé responds first with a beautiful letter. Unfortunately, I fear that the comic aspect of the book has escaped him, more impressed as he is by its cravenness even though I see the systematization of such a sensibility as a technique of humor. Michel sends me a note that delights me in seeming to have taken into account what I wanted to put into the text. Next I have the pleasure of listening to him speak about it on the couch at rue de Vaugirard as he quotes various phrases, laughing again at having remembered them. I love his laughs even if, more than any of them, it's the little one he inevitably has when he opens the door of the apartment to me.

Bolstered by these initial reactions, I leave the manuscript with my father. I have always thought I'd write and that my father would publish it, and the two things were really just one— that is, if I ever managed finishing a manuscript I liked enough to submit to him. Well no, it turns out that these two actions are completely separate from each other.

My father has a thousand reservations about the manuscript, and none of them seem to be literary to me. What the family might think of it takes sudden precedence. As a teenager, I'm both satisfied about having pushed my father, allegedly so open, to the breaking point—I see it as a success—and disgusted that so tolerant a man isn't admitting that this is precisely what has happened, that the quality of the book, struggling to become one, has nothing to do with his reticence. On the contrary, the more I expect him to admit this, the more he refuses. Honesty has its mysteries.

Michel is at the heart of our confrontation. My father and he are the only two people of that age with whom I'm close. It feels strange to speak about my father to Michel in that way on rue de Vaugirard, in this world so far away from my family's conventions. Despite my rancor, I'm glad to sense my father's presence in this place, be it only through my reports of our conversations.

One evening I come to see Michel at rue de Vaugirard and he asks me if I've read the story that appeared in *Gai Pied*, which publishes one a week. No, its pullout sentence in big letters was so lame that it didn't seem like the whole of it would be worth its weight. Michel says that that sentence was so bad that he wanted to read the complete text to see if it was really the best it had to offer, and that was the case. I'm sitting on the couch with the paper in my hands, Michel next to me in order to read over my shoulder, and what a wonderful moment. The story is so bottom of the barrel that you'd have to call it a sketch. Even the title is a mistake, and every sentence is worse than the other. You couldn't laugh more if you were peaking on LSD. Michel is so doubled up with laughter that he falls off the couch and slides onto the floor, which worries me for a moment without my being able to do anything about it, given my own fit of laughter, which is making my muscles unable to function. I love the fact that writing is clinching such incredible closeness.

This is the time of desire. My manuscript is a partisan of pleasure, and that's one facet of it that Michel likes. We spend an evening discussing it. I detest the idea of desire as a weapon, the way some boys see it as the diamond in them, an island of purity in an ocean of alienation. In the backrooms where I go regularly, I have sex with people whom I might not desire if I could see them, but who give me great pleasure in darkness. What is more, these backrooms furnish an amusing situation: I had my money stolen from the pocket of my skin-tight jeans (and that's certainly not amusing) because those jeans, which were around my ankles with my underpants, weren't at all skin-tight any more. There's something entertaining about imagining a boy on all fours in the dark in the middle of all that forni-cating, looking not for sex but for all pants around ankles and what's in their pockets. Michel also pointed out to me that I hadn't had any desire for LSD—because how would I have been able to without knowing what it was? It's the pleasure of the drug that creates the desire for it. The entire rue de Vaugirard is an education of that order. Regarding the backrooms, I didn't tell him that I may not have changed my habits, but at least my sexual positions, because of the "gay cancer" the press is men-tioning—my never-ending cautiousness.

I appoint Michel arbitrator of my quarrel with my father. Of course, he only receives his information from me but is big enough to take that into account. It's resolved without his ever having pronounced a word against my father, neither against the man himself nor against his image for a son. It's easier for him to tell the difference between the father and the publisher than it is for my father and me. Eventually my father does publish the manuscript after having had it read anonymously by his usual adviser, whose opinion—warmly shared with me by that person—delights me. Everything is settled, but my father still insists on publishing the book under a pseudonym. I've offered the manu-script elsewhere, and no one wanted it, so I don't have a choice. However, using a pseudonym under such duress seems grotesque to me. Surprised at first by this umpteenth development, Michel ratifies it in his way. At another dinner on rue de Vaugirard, as I'm coming in, he tosses an unknown name at me, asking me what I think of it. I don't think anything, not understanding it. It's the pseudonym he's concocted for me about which he explains the ins and outs that escaped me. I enthusiastically adopt it, and even my father finds nothing more to say about it.

6

Michel invites me to come and take LSD with Monsieur Marc at three on Wednesday afternoon. "Monsieur Marc" is what Michel calls a boy our age with whom he has fallen in love, resulting in our hearing a lot about him without having ever yet seen him. We also know he has no qualms about drugs since, despite the fact that he has never tried acid, he's more familiar with heroin than any of us are. One evening, Michel tells Hervé and me how he met him. He'd noticed his beauty among the student body of his course at the Collège de France, open to everybody as the institution wanted. Hervé and I have always had the feeling that going to the class wouldn't please Michel. But Michel is delighted that this particular boy came. It entertains him to entertain us by describing the way he approached him. He didn't know how to go about it. So when the boy at the end of class came to pick up his tape recorder from the table where he'd placed it to record the course as many do, Michel claims not having found anything better to say to start a conversation than something like, "Oh, what an attractive tape recorder." Making us laugh makes him laugh, too, not to mention the joy he experiences in noting that at least there's one situation in which he doesn't seem smarter than us.

Monsieur Marc is heterosexual, lives with a girl and makes us dislike him immediately given the way he treats Michel. He schedules or accepts meetings he doesn't show up for, drops out of sight and then pops up abruptly, but disappears again in the same way. He's totally devoid of dependability—like one of my lovers. One time, when he overdoes this, Didier has the bright idea of publishing a personals ad in *Libération*, a paper the boy reads: "Michel's friends think that Monsieur Marc has gone too far." All of us are more or less dismayed, fearing that Michel might take it badly, but he thinks it's fun; and it's effective, so we can take our dismay and be gone with it. My only fear is that, with or without warning, Monsieur Marc actually won't come to rue de Vaugirard and that we'll have to wait for hours before deciding what to do to make a serious point of his absence, as I always do when somebody stands me up. Even so, he's already there when Michel opens the door for me. He's very handsome, and I'm all the more happy to see him because we immediately hit it off. Michel is far from shy when it comes to putting others at ease.

There are three hits of acid left from a stash. We've already taken a great number of hits from it without a problem. Despite that, several dozen minutes after ingesting the last three, it becomes clear that they're unusually potent. We're ripped to the gills as never before, despite a certain reserve provoked by that same potency. We're used to going with the flow, but this time it's a matter of giving in to the high on a different scale, as if our usual personality were being attacked with real violence. I'm stretched out on the couch, and Michel and Monsieur Marc are each in an armchair when Michel suddenly stands, puts on a jacket and leaves the apartment. His face looked ravaged. With the extra-lucidity of the acid, that incomprehensible power it gives you to read the features of your fellow trippers, I can't do otherwise than take note that something is happening that shouldn't be—something dire. Monsieur Marc is startled by Michel's departure, not to mention its suddenness. Proud as I am of my competence with acid, I tell the neophyte in a few words not to worry. This takes a toll on me yet doesn't—doesn't, because I'm persuaded that's what I ought to say and, ideally, what I ought to do; yet does, because I'm incredibly worried about the state Michel's in and anxious about the chain of events still to come this afternoon. But I cling to the conviction born of my knowledge (it isn't for nothing that I've taken so much acid, and my greed for it is justified by the intuitions it brings) that we mustn't dwell on Michel during the storm, because it's of no use to him and can only drag Monsieur Marc and me down too. We have to postpone our worry for another time when we'll be able to be reasonable. For the moment, whatever our concerns are, we cannot worry about him now.

I'm on the razor's edge and can't stop thinking about it—in acid's hurricane where streams are layered in my head, blending their contents. Monsieur Marc is no more full of vim and vigor than I am, something strikingly obvious. Never has the apartment looked like this: no longer anything in it I can hang on to, not the Mahler corner nor the door, which is a wall all by itself, nor any memory. We are in a permanent state of emergency. At each instant all that's necessary is to find a way to go without harm to the next instant, and these instants are eternal. I don't know how I'm going to get out of this unless by not thinking about it. Shifting my eyes forty-five degrees to the left toward Monsieur Marc is a movement and demands effort, but whether physical or mental I can't determine. He senses when I look at him and looks back, unless it wasn't he who started this and it wasn't because I was attracted by his eyes that mine have turned toward him. In any case, when I see him, I recognize the state Monsieur Marc is in at this tenth or hundredth of a second. If I notice that he's doing well, I prolong my glance to feed on the refuge it provides; in the opposite case, I shorten it in order not to be contaminated by his despair, at any rate not daring to look at him except when I think the face I'm displaying is acceptable and my own anxiety is under control. I'm convinced that if one of us founders the other won't be able to resist. Generosity requires the most absolute selfishness, too.

It's also my job to carry out the practical tasks of our session. Faced with Monsieur Marc, who doesn't hear that a record is finished and that you need to put on another, I'm the only one capable of taking on the job with infinite care, my clumsiness magnified tenfold by the drug, because he's unaware that it's at least necessary to try to punctuate this infinite time while the acid is passing through us as we wait for the moment when it has passed, when it will be possible to reflect more seriously, to think about Michel.

The telephone in the living room rings, something that hasn't happened in such a situation, because Gérard is supposed to disconnect it during those times. I'm forced to answer. It's Éric, the boy I fell in love with a few months ago. Our desires were different, but he knew how to see to it that this wouldn't hinder our connection, something for which I'm especially grateful seeing that he's only twenty years old. It makes his capacity for relating seem that much more remarkable. Although my feelings for him are far from having ended, and even though they're not that strong because I still haven't been able to get over the mind and body of Valentin despite the fact that I never saw him again, fifteen days ago Éric fell in love with another boy. He's calling after things just went badly with him, and he feels lost. He'd like to stop by. Since he and I have taken several acid trips together, he's aware of the state it puts you in; but because he still wants to come over, he must—I can only say yes. Not to mention that I just don't have the heart to feel jealous or anything of that order when what's preoccupying me is on a scale without comparison. Lovers come and go, but Michel is there for eternity.

Miraculously, without any significant comedown, we're awarded some respite, since the strongest of the acid's effect is finally behind us. Because I'm experienced, I can infallibly recognize the moment when you can take heroin without danger, tipping more smoothly into part two of the trip. What is more, when it comes to a drug for which he has a lot more competence than me, Monsieur Marc feels at ease, even if he can't inject it as he's used to doing. He has ended up obeying my urgings not to think about Michel. His ignorance about acid and therefore about what Michel is risking has made it easier for him. Now he's enjoying being in Michel's apartment, a rare experience for him; and his increasingly joyous mood carries me along with it. I make two thick lines and snort mine with the McDonald's straw, there for that purpose, and then I hand the straw to Monsieur Marc. But I didn't do a very good job of blowing my nose previously, and the straw is full of snot—which is disgusting. Monsieur Marc holds it under water to clean it. When he comes back with a wet straw, it turns out it was a stupid idea. The heroin is going to fasten to the moisture on the plastic, and it will be unsnortable. We try to dry off the straw by blowing through it, by threading a handkerchief through it, any piece of fabric that isn't very thick—all to no avail if you ignore the fact that this is the best moment of the afternoon because it sends us into gales of laughter, until Monsieur Marc takes out a bill from his pocket and rolls it into a straw. Such an ordinary solution that took us so long to discover produces another burst of laughter. Things are going better, at least for us two.

Éric arrives during another weaker phase of the acid, allowing me to explain the situation to him in a few words. It's what he needed, and it's obvious that just being here does him good. But Monsieur Marc and I plunge little by little into a new acid attack after the last respite, like besieged men forced to go off to battle again. Over the long run we've become drained, our energy consumed by both the acid itself and the energy spent resisting it. We hear a key turning in the lock. Then the door opens and Michel appears accompanied by a guy we don't know who's closer to his age than ours. What now? Michel still seems unwell, although somewhat less. And who is this guy?

The man asks for a glass of water, which Michel, still silent, needs to use to swallow a pill. In fact, the acid we took is still in a deceptively intense phase. The unfamiliar man has made a bad impression on me from the first moment, and now it's confirmed. Barely has he finished speaking when what is doubtlessly a new effect of my extra-lucidity makes me see it as an attempt at murder or assisted suicide. Thinking the pill is a way of putting an end to Michel, I remain frozen in place, full of hostility. Monsieur Marc seems to me to be in the same state of mind. Éric has discreetly stayed in one corner, out of my view. I've always had a mind that goes off on a tangent in every sense, but one thing is certain: my immobility is an expression of aggression, indicating that this guy isn't going to be able to count on us for his dirty work. I don't know if I'm communicating it, but I feel like a sulking child, arms crossed to make it clear that he won't obey.

The tension of the scene transforms me into a bubble, or lake, of anxiety. I instantly feel like those characters in comic strips or cartoons who wring out their clothes after a scare because they're so soaked with sweat. I'm made of water, a statue of water whose body and bones could be wrung out. I can't imagine a situation more horrible than the one I'm seeing: someone I love is asking me for a vital favor and I'm incapable of doing it for him. It's an inverted fantasy, pure perversity. I think Michel wants me to do something, and I don't know what day it is, couldn't even tell the time. I'm in control of absolutely nothing. It's as if he were being carried away by a vortex, holding out a hand that I'd only need to grasp to save him, but a cramp, or I don't know what, over which I have no power is specifically preventing me from doing it.

"Where's the kitchen?" the guy asks. No one answers. Michel points to it, and when the other guy comes back with the glass, he swallows his pill and heads for his room to go to bed. The stranger leaves without our having exchanged a word.

We took the acid at the very beginning of the afternoon, so the heat of August and bright light are still present. Monsieur Marc and I are in the living room, feeling somewhat disoriented, and Michel is sleeping in the next room. Éric is in our room, but our trip is making us nearly impossible to communicate with. Both of us try to come back to Earth, but our struggle continues despite the effect of the heroin. Never have I been confronted by acid this strong.

All of a sudden, Michel comes out of his room in his underpants. He's always so discreet that this sight alone makes me worry again, despite the fact that the vortex is gone and Michel wasn't swept away. He recounts the features of what happened to him, and I have the impression of being alone with him as he does, isolated from Monsieur Marc and Éric, who has never seen him before. At one moment he was so unwell that he decided to go to a neighborhood doctor who was seeing patients and whom he knew a little. The waiting room was full, and he was shut up there among the old ladies and children who comprise the majority of afternoon cases. Even in the middle of an acid trip that's going fantastically, such a situation is enough to become a downer—pronto. I don't know how Michel could have done it. He calls himself heroic, a word so startling in his mouth I immediately believe him. That's the only explanation for such conduct. Michel immediately tempers the term, recounting that the doctor, when he opened the door, understood that something wasn't going well and had him come into his office first. That allowed Michel to explain things, and the doctor prescribed a strong sedative. Between the doctor's and the pharmacy, he sat down on a bench, and just at that moment a guy he knew passed by and certainly must have also noticed something, because Michel was truly relieved when this unknown person (but not to him) went with him to the pharmacy and then to the apartment.

He goes back to bed. The telephone in the studio rings. It's Daniel, who knew we were going to take acid and wants some news. The only way I can respond is to tell him it hasn't gone well and that it would be better for him to come over. He arrives very quickly. I sum things up for him as coherently as I can, and Daniel goes to see Michel in his room. He's reassured when he comes out. Then it seems to take an infinite amount of time to tell him about the acid, going back to explain certain details when Monsieur Marc doesn't, clarifying points over and over. When I come to the affair of the glass of water and the pill, Éric comments (without any ill will because he knows acid) that we were ridiculous, turning a glass of water into the affair of the century. So I explain again what I was thinking, and so does Monsieur Marc, and there's no end to it. Meanwhile Éric is on the phone, managing to reach his new love. He leaves while we're still at it. His pleasure infects us—finally some good news after such a tough day. It's late when Daniel says he's going to sleep on rue de Vaugirard, and Monsieur Marc and I finally hit the street.

We have just as much need to walk as to talk. It's nearly dark now. I walk Monsieur Marc to his apartment, miles away. I've always seen acid as a creator of intimacy. Wow, how much more it is when it happens under such difficult circumstances! Monsieur Marc and I are now close, two people who at lunchtime hadn't even seen each other yet. Leaving him makes me feel abandoned, and I don't want to go back to my place where loneliness will weigh heavier, so I keep walking. I come to a club where I sometimes go but never at this hour. I have no desire for a boy. It's just that, despite my fatigue, I have too much energy, and I'm thinking too hard. The only thing in my head is obsessive thoughts about Michel. Because it's time to close, they throw me out of the club. There's no other solution but to return to my place, but by making detours, wasting time on benches. The sun has risen. I have a message on my answering machine recorded at two in the morning in which Éric tells me all goes well as far as he's concerned. I wasn't thinking about him, but it makes me happy that's he's reappearing this way. There are some hang-ups after that message, giving the impression that Michel called with the strength to speak to me but not to my answering machine. I go to bed even though it's obvious I'll have trouble sleeping. I don't unplug the phone in case I do fall asleep, in hopes of being awakened by a telephone call from Michel, which I expect to arrive as soon as he's in shape.

These hours are a nightmare. The pernicious effects of the acid aren't lessened but increased by the heroin, which has also become unpleasant. The curtains in my room are enemies. There is some kind of hostility in them that I can't detect. I know that it's a hallucination, a form of madness, but that doesn't change anything about it, the same way I get scared watching a bloody horror film when I know they are only actors on the screen and the blood is gooseberry jam. The only way to struggle against this assault is to keep my eyes open, because everything rages when I close them for an instant. My sole method for keeping the curtains at a distance is to keep staring at them. Naturally I want to sleep, now. Just to close my eyes. It's becoming impossible to keep my eyelids raised, a physical effort, a mental effort, a kind of hell.

I'm not even thinking about the ordinary pleasant day it might have been if I hadn't added heroin to the acid, or taken the acid itself. But the situation is what it is. The drug unfurls around me, materializes into menacing depictions that I can only believe even if I don't believe in them. That is what a hallucination is—an error of analysis that's impossible to correct, a disability. With my gift for worry, I dread the moments when keeping my eyes open will no longer be enough to safeguard me from it.

The telephone rings, and Michel sounds good, so I'm reassured. Since he's inviting me over, I run to rue de Vaugirard under the pretext of lunching or breakfasting with him, despite the hour it is, so we can talk and be together. Michel is less lively than usual, and there are still remnants of the acid experience in his face. Nevertheless, he cheerfully recounts that the friend he brought to his place yesterday whom Monsieur Marc and I treated so strangely thought we were two hustlers who just wanted to get out of the trap in which they'd accidentally landed. It makes me happy that someone thinks others are ready to pay to go to bed with me.

For a long time I'd been planning to leave this weekend for Normandy for a family vacation. I stick to the plan but return Sunday afternoon. I stop by for dinner on rue de Vaugirard at an ungodly hour, too early; and contrary to practice, Michel takes me to a restaurant close by. Contrary to practice as well, he talks about his work, the book he's writing. Neither he nor I have regained our normal state. It's still very early when we leave the restaurant, and Michel drops me off by car at the bar where I usually go, as if he's ashamed of spoiling the evening by finishing it at that hour. I've barely set foot in the bar when I recognize Valentin, the boy I've been running after for two years and whom I met there for that first and only night we spent together. The object of my love is with three boys. I come up to them, to him, look at him in a way that makes Valentin notice me, and I can see that he doesn't recognize me. So I mention our night together, but his companions scoff at its insignificance, as if there were hundreds of such partners and desertions. I don't get flustered and speak instead of our endless phone calls and missed meetings. Suddenly he remembers who I am. Lucidity? Clairvoyance? Mistake? I'm persuaded that, one way or another, I count for him.

The next day, when I tell Michel everything, that I didn't spend the night with Valentin but that we're supposed to have lunch together the day after tomorrow, Michel asks me to promise him I'll give Valentin up for good if he doesn't show up this time. "He can still miss one date, can't he?" I answer pathetically, emphasizing that number because I can no more get rid of the boy than go back on a promise to Michel.

7

"I've heard a lot about you," says Michel to Valentin, who has been saving that line for himself when I take him to dine for the first time on rue de Vaugirard. One evening when we're arguing, since I must at least teach him an implicit lesson, Valentin answers, having been informed by me about my family, that he can tell I'm the grandson of a prosecutor. That leaves an impression on me straightaway and particularly the next day at Michel's. I'm giving him the latest news about the problems my father is creating for my second novel, the fact that he'd like to keep using my pseudonym. I'd accepted the first time as a compromise, not for it to have any effect on the future. Michel himself is surprised, thinks that my father is going too far. Bitterly I imagine that my father is jealous of writers, of not writing. Michel doesn't believe it for a second. My father's irritation, he adds, quoting one of my father's former authors, is set off instead by the fact that when you speak with him about such things he wants to create the feeling of his acting as an intermediary for a court composed of all the prestigious authors he publishes. I judge it necessary to change publishers and that way of making judgments. My future is no longer subject to my father's house. When he speaks to me about what will happen to the publishing company after his death, I know he's expecting me to respond, so I say something else.

When I come over to rue de Vaugirard Michel tells me about reading an article in *Le Monde* that afternoon, written on the occasion of the anniversary of the death of a musician with whom he was close. The article points out the composer's flaws, which explains why he lacks a larger recognition even today. Michel says he was convinced of it for a few moments, before being ashamed of his reaction. It is rare for him to feel such affinity. He has already told me that death is an event you can't take in immediately, but at least it has the advantage of making the survivor master of the relationship, something that will no longer evolve except inside you. I feel a strange connection to our conversation, blended as it is with intelligence and affection. Sometimes I take all he tells me as information even if I'm having trouble deciphering it, sometimes nothing.

Knowing how close I am to Michel, my brother brags about how lucky I am. I know, I answer, and I tell him how I rely on Michel every time I'm in love. He thinks I could make better use of such a friend. I have, without the words to explain it.

Michel has no trip in view, no occasion for loaning the rue de Vaugirard to a gang in the near future. In any case, acid is over, at least in Paris. In Paris, we can only take it on rue de Vaugirard, and I don't feel like taking any and going back to the way my head was the last time. For a while I've been trying it at times in Normandy when I leave for the weekend with someone for the property my grandparents own up there. Once with Gérard, where we meet somebody else named Hervé whom I know from childhood and adolescence but haven't seen in years. Like Monsieur Marc, he has such a familiarity with drugs through heroin that he's capable of spending a good part of an acid trip with his parents without a hitch. And with Éric, who suddenly kneels in front of me to retie my shoes to the astonishment of my cousins, who are confronted by my homosexuality in that way. And now with Valentin, where it becomes an intense experience with good and bad moments. Something has changed since the acid has been eighty-sixed from rue de Vaugirard, something has happened. Even so, we get back the apartment for a few days, and we have nothing but good times there.

Sometimes Michel organizes little parties, for example, the one with the Japanese dancer. Once it's in honor of an American photographer whom Hervé adores, as well as for the catalogue of his exhibition for which Michel is writing a preface. And this is a chance for Hervé and me to be invited together again to rue de Vaugirard. At the beginning, it was happening a lot, but we acted so stupid together that even Michel had trouble bearing it and for a time preferred to have each of us over separately. One evening when all three of us were having dinner in the kitchen, the telephone rang in the living room, and Michel was busy, so Hervé went to answer it. There are two phone lines on rue de Vaugirard. The one in the studio is unlisted, and that's the one Michel answers. The other, in the living room, remains unplugged most of the time, which is convenient because it allows me to plug it in and give my number at rue de Vaugirard without risking it bothering Michel too much when he gets back. It was also plugged in the day of this dinner, and Hervé comes back to tell Michel in a mocking voice that when he asked who was calling a young, masculine voice had answered, "A good friend of Michel." Michel goes to it and returns five minutes later to tell us that it really was a friend. "A good friend but one who had the wrong number," says Hervé because we're just as much pests as we are stupid.

This time the evening is for William Burroughs. A film on him is coming out, and the director and his subject are on rue de

Vaugirard, along with the person who did the subtitles for the film, the good friend of Michel who didn't have the right number. Like Michel, I've been lovers with this boy, who nevertheless irritates me because he's always such a yes man, which obliges me to push my provocation a little further when I want to rile him. Moreover Michel questioned me about this point before confessing that it's the same for him, that he'd been just as irritated. And he told me that he'd asked a former lover of the boy why they'd separated, who answered that it was because the boy was impossible, always contradicting every point he made. During the entire evening, despite our liking Burroughs's work, Hervé and I keep to ourselves, speaking to no one other than Michel, who is otherwise occupied in making sure that everything is going as well as possible. As for me, I've always felt the others aren't taking advantage of the rue de Vaugirard as much as they could and that they ought to, even if it's less welcoming on these occasions for me as well.

"Hervé is the only person I know who can say, 'I just read a wonderful book. It's called *The Charterhouse of Parma* (*La Chartreuse de Parme*),'" says Michel to me with evident pleasure. The compliment is striking because of its tone. Never, in any case, would he ever say a word to me against Hervé. Even though Hervé had loved writing a screenplay with Patrice Chéreau and things were spoiled when the screenplay was finished and it was time to shoot, Michel isn't taking Hervé's side, as I would have guessed, but keeping the scale balanced. In a work he's always sensitive to the nature of the author's relationship to it, and in my eyes this almost becomes a determining factor. When the film is finished, Michel, not intending a critique but an observation, returns to that youthful necessity, Hervé's difficulty in tolerating dispossession. Although suddenly dispossession seems to be one of Michel's interests, he's talking about self-effacement, and on several occasions he mentions it like an objective.

One evening I'm on rue de Vaugirard for less than three minutes when he places the second Pléiade volume of *Memoirs from Beyond the Grave* (*Les Mémoires d'outre-tombe*) between my hands. It opens after the death of Napoleon, when Chateaubriand expresses how much he misses that eminent adversary and how he now finds himself in so lackluster a world. "In expressing myself about our lack of value, I kept my conscience pressed close; I wondered whether I hadn't incorporated myself into these nullified times out of an ulterior motive, in order to acquire the right to condemn the others; persuaded as I was *in petto*[1] that my name was being read in the midst of all these erasures. No: I am convinced that we're all vanishing: firstly, because inside us we don't have what is needed to live; secondly, because the century in which we are beginning or finishing our days no longer itself has what is needed to make us live." What Michel liked the most in this passage was the word *erasures*.[2] I'm struck by the conviction that he's putting more into this than Chateaubriand.

For him, the relationship that Hervé and I have is a love relationship. Fine with me. Since I've managed to have some, I've always felt that my ordeals during a passionate relationship come in large part from social conventions with which I actually have nothing to do, that my jealousy is an exterior construct, that a pitiful vision of pride doesn't suit me. By his irresistible kindness and intelligence, Michel is creating another world around him, inventing new bonds of love and sex, bodies and feelings. I truly

---

1. Translator's note: (from the Italian) "secretly" or "privately"
2. Translator's note: The French word with this meaning is actually one that no longer appears in standard French dictionaries: *effaçures*.

don't understand where it's leading me if not toward a sort of salvation whose precise delineations I can't see. My relationship with Michel as well is a lover's relationship.

At several dinners, Michel has coughing fits for which he excuses himself. They complicate his conversation. Sometimes he's tired out from medical exams, and it might happen when we're in the living room that he doesn't hear the telephone ringing in the studio, which I try to signal to him gently, without making much of it in my mind. Late one afternoon, he calls me to dine with him, as I do often when I'm in bad shape and need his company. I already have something planned. I telephone the boy to cancel. He's not a friend, just a young man who is ill and who is not someone anybody should be happy about dining with, so much so that he's a master at conducting one of those thirteenth-hour conversations over the telephone before I can even speak a word, expressing how happy he is about seeing me and about the fact that he has everything ready, which ends up keeping me from canceling the evening. I call back Michel, who wasn't expecting me to fail, and in his voice I sense a disappointment that makes the dinner with the boy a nightmare for me. I remember another disappointment, one evening when I was telling Michel how acid triggers questions you wouldn't ever ask yourself in a normal frame of mind, thereby giving rise to a different way of thinking. He asked me to describe some, and he didn't find my answer as interesting as he was hoping it would be.

Michel is usually so discreet about his work that I'm always especially attentive when he mentions it, which he does more frequently now that the end of his infinite books is approaching. I can sense his joy when he refers to what he calls his seamstress' work, after a book is finished and all there are to do are little touch-ups that are crucial, when there is no longer anything left but details that aren't right, little nothings that are enough to keep everything from working, although all of it is close to being finished. One evening he tells me that the books he's been working on year after year are finished and what great pleasure such an achievement brings him. But he says that when he stood up from the table where he'd pronounced that end in his head, he knocked over a glass and broke it, making him think that—wouldn't you know it—the time for satisfaction was already over. It had only lasted a few seconds.

During our quarrel, my father stopped publishing the review I was editing. At first Michel had been surprised that I was no longer struggling with it, especially since the review seemed to be doing better than ever in a literary sense. Then he took back his surprise, musing that you always lose some of your enthusiasm concentrating on something that isn't working after it begins to work over the course of time. Today, he tells me that the subjects he was bringing up in his own work did not interest anyone in the past, and that now everyone seems passionate about them. His tone is one of regret.

My brother makes a long animated film. I go with Michel to a screening, and he adores the film. At our dinners I take advantage of this to tell him a thousand things about my brother. That evening, after having seen my brother that afternoon, I tell Michel that my brother didn't see animation as a calling. On the contrary he feels as if he could have done something completely different. It interests Michel much more than I would have thought. He thinks he himself has only written books by chance.

The release of *The Use of Pleasure* (*L'Usage des plaisirs*) and *The Care of the Self* (*Le Souci de soi*), the second and third volumes of his *History of Sexuality* (*Histoire de la sexualité*), is making him a bit anxious. He's taken on a subject for which he possessed no scholarly credentials before starting to work, and he's hearing increasingly obvious rumors that make him fear established specialists might use it for a hatchet job. It's always the same: we can't understand why people aren't rejoicing at the appearance of his new books, why they don't see them as an opportunity. For some time he has driven home the fact to me that you're losing your time in wanting to appease certain enemies because what people don't like is not so much what you do as what you are. He's heard that Untel has said such things against him, demolishing his work before even having read it. Untel happens to be a friend of my father whom I tell about it, expressing my surprise at the behavior of a friend who is always so blameless. "I'm going to find out about it," says my father, whose ambition has always been to add Michel's name to his catalogue. My father calls me back, having apparently sorted out the affair. Untel will no longer take the risk of batting an eyelash. I report this to Michel, and shortly after, Hervé tells me how touched Michel was by my intervention. I'm surprised and miffed with myself. I would do a million times more than that for Michel. Why hasn't he been persuaded of it for the last several hundred years?

8

For each period of time, there has been a fixed evening in the week when I go to dine on rue de Vaugirard, in addition to those evenings that pop up spontaneously. Right now it happens on Sundays. In the afternoon, because I still have no news from Michel and am not at my place, I call him because our understanding is also to confirm what has no need to be. He answers and tells me that it's good that I called. He needs to cancel this evening because he doesn't feel well and is going to the hospital. He doesn't convey any worry, and my wish not to be worried about him when I can't do anything about it has survived our last acid trip.

He doesn't answer the telephone during the day on Monday so I call Daniel. He seems more anxious, and the truth is that so am I. Michel was sick at his place on Sunday, and there's no information about what the problem is. Daniel makes a remark about the state I was in yesterday evening. I don't understand. Actually, he had called me yesterday evening and didn't reach me. When he asked to speak to me some boy laughed in his face; and prompted by habit, he figured I was in the middle of an acid trip. He isn't aware that the days of Parisian acid trips are over. I correct his mistaken impression— he dialed the wrong number, obviously—but he still doesn't understand how I could know that Michel is in the hospital. I explain. He's happy to discover from my account that Michel himself had agreed to be hospitalized.

The hospital is two métro stations away from rue de Vaugirard. It's hot. Michel is lying in boxer shorts and a T-shirt, and he doesn't get up. When he realizes that one of his balls is slipping from his shorts, he embarrassedly adjusts it. All of that makes me anxious.

He is transferred to the Hôpital de la Pitié-Salpêtrière, which doesn't seem to augur well, either, even if it is nearer my place. Unlike a private hospital, there's no television. Hervé and I offer to take on the task of renting one so that at least he can watch the Roland-Garros finals on Sunday. We joke around. All four of us are together with Daniel, and it's a pleasant afternoon.

There's no longer any question of a television and Roland-Garros since McEnroe, Michel's favorite, has lost after having been inches from winning. I see it as an appalling sign. He's now in intensive care. Apart from Daniel, whom we call daily, visits are narrowly controlled. Moreover, you can only enter the room covered entirely in plastic, from feet and hands to head. According to what Daniel tells me, the doctors aren't very forthcoming or informed about details, but it's easy to see that things aren't taking a good turn. Nevertheless, I manage not to dwell on it. I've learned to fight my anxiety about Michel. I only let in what I have to. In the hospital's sunny garden, as Daniel describes the poor state in which he has just seen Michel, his worry about his not regaining all his faculties, I muster all my argumentative imagination to reassure him, so effectively that it spreads to me. "I understand why Michel loves you so much," he thanks me. And in this light the sunny garden is magnificent.

However, there are other days when Daniel isn't doing well and I comfort him by telephone. Sometimes he envies Hervé's and my relationship with Michel—its light-heartedness—as if he himself weren't up to par in that respect. Because I know enough about Michel's love for Daniel, it's easy to oppose such implausible humility. On the other hand, given Michel's current state, I'm grateful to Daniel for expressing this as a tribute that only he himself could offer to the relationship Hervé and I have been able to foster with his lover.

News of Michel's illness has gotten out to *Libération*. They're talking about AIDS, as are Hervé and I, although the word is never mentioned with Daniel until the day he calls to tell me that the doctor has assured him "it's not AIDS." I hang up the phone crazy with joy. All I ask from life is the life of Michel.

I go back to my place for an after-lunch meeting with Gérard. There's a worrisome message from Daniel on my answering machine, asking me to come to the hospital right away. I ask Gérard to wait for me. I'm afraid Michel is dead. Out of fear that the bus might be caught in traffic, and without thinking that the hospital Pitié-Salpêtrière is three métro stops away, I start running, so urgent did Daniel's message seem. I arrive sweating. Since I can find my way around the buildings now without a problem, I reach the right floor. I'm not allowed into the hallway, but I can see black mourning crepe outside Michel's room. Daniel comes to meet me and announce the disaster. From his pocket he takes an envelope containing the will that was found on rue de Vaugirard and has me read it as he praises Michel's generosity. His generosity toward Daniel seems like the most natural thing in the world to me. The will has a strikingly under-stated strength, but due to my gift for angst, I'm worried about leaving certain questions hanging. I approve of everything Daniel says. He takes me into the room and draws back discreetly, imagining that I want to be alone with Michel one last time. I don't. I didn't choose to be alone with a corpse, and my grief takes the form of feeling ill at ease.

It turns out that I don't have to stay alone in the room because a friend of Michel enters, someone I've never seen but whom he has already spoken about. One of her grandmothers, a great lady from Prussia, was once in a train compartment when a field officer entered and politely asked if it would bother her if he smoked. Michel really loved her answer: "I don't know. Nobody has ever smoked in front of me." The granddaughter explains to Daniel and indirectly to me that she sensed something, that it seemed to her that she should come at once to the hospital. To me this feels like indiscretion, but since her being there seems to soothe Daniel, I stifle my negative frame of mind once more.

I'm alone with her in front of the body. She asks me if it's the first close death I've been confronted with, and after my yes, says that I'll see, I'll get used to it, that you can live with it. I'm like an adolescent stricken by his first experience of suffering from love and it's being explained to him that it's no big deal, whereas I can't see anything more important that could possibly happen to me. A kind of repressed rage toward that woman grips me. This isn't the case of some love-struck teenager elevating the object of his affection sky-high. It's Michel who has died, and anyone should be able to understand that this calamity isn't an ordinary one, the result of some pipe dream about a friend I'll be able to replace with ten others. She speaks gently to me, takes me with her by car to the exit of the hospital, but when we've reached the boulevard drops me off to figure things out on my own, adding to her arrears.

I find Gérard at the house where I have some heroin. We snort some to deaden the blow. I call Hervé because I want to tell him not to end up involuntarily alone in the room with Michel's body as happened to me. Suddenly this seems very important to me, but I can't reach him. I call Thierry with the news, and also Monsieur Marc, whom I haven't spoken to since we parted at the end of our lengthy walk in the middle of the night during the last acid trip. Daniel has asked me to make both calls to let them know, and he himself has made others. It has been decided not to make the information public before Michel's brother arrives in the provinces to tell their mother at her home. Hervé calls to ask if he can come by and does. Being in Michel's room didn't weigh on him in the same way. He leaves very soon.

For several months, on Monday evenings I've been hosting a radio broadcast for young people. Michel even took the trouble of listening to it and advising me on the way to modulate my voice. Gérard has co-hosted it with me, then our friend Marc, and tonight with Valentin there are four of us. This is the last place I'd like to be, much less be clowning around, which is what we like to do on the radio, but I can't imagine doing otherwise. Valentin, who is an actor, although he's never had a role, has also attached some importance to this program, as if it could help him with his career. Somehow the broadcast happens. In fact, it isn't the worst thing to have your mind concentrating on something else. I only needed to warn the sound engineer that a friend had died and that therefore I was in a certain mood so that he wouldn't toss out any kind of challenge to me, as he sometimes playfully does. It is past one in the morning when we leave the studio. I don't want to sleep alone. I want to spend the night with Valentin, to whom I've told nothing, faithful as I've been to the discretion Daniel demanded a little while ago. I especially don't want to pressure him. If he sleeps over, it mustn't be because Michel is dead—although, yes, maybe that's the reason that I want him so much. He refuses. I reproach him for it by phone the next morning after having read the papers paying homage to Michel. He maintains that he'd found out Michel had died, and because I didn't speak about it, he didn't know if I was aware of it and was therefore uncomfortable with the idea of sharing that night with me. I'm convinced of the validity of his motive, but it's no challenge to the fact that it was inappropriate to abandon me that evening, inappropriate in terms of our relationship, independently of ethics. It brings up the stupid incident that happened to me a month ago. Michel had had his new books sent to me, and when I dined that evening on rue de Vaugirard, I didn't bring them with me so that it wouldn't seem like I was asking for a dedication. And Michel, thinking it natural I would come with them, had been sorry, telling me he did want to write me a dedication, and it had become obvious to me that he already knew what he wanted to write. I never saw him again except at the hospital, a place where I wasn't going to burden him with something like that.

After going with Daniel to the hospital to take care of some formalities, Hervé comes over in the evening and tells me he has seen some articles. Valentin and I are watching the final Euro football match between France and Spain on television. Because Hervé needs to speak to me, we go into my office. He announces that Michel has officially died from AIDS. Valentin interrupts us with the news that the French have just scored the goal that will make their win a sure thing and wants to know whether I want to come and see it in slow motion. No. He leaves. I don't know what to say to Hervé. I don't give one good goddamn about what Michel died of. Since it just happened the day before yesterday, it's all I'm thinking about. But what about the doctors? Why have they spoken since they weren't allowed to say anything? I feel the same resentment I felt for the granddaughter of the woman whom no one had ever smoked in front of, the one who didn't take me all the way to my place.

Hervé and I are spending the evening with Daniel. He's telling us about the service. The funeral will take place in the morning at the mortuary, then the corpse will be transferred to the village where Michel's mother lives to be buried there. Several people will come there by car, and we won't have any problem getting the vehicles. A flower wreath will be buried with Michel with the words, "Since Michel's life was endowed not only with love but also with friendship." Daniel has decided it will be inscribed with our three first names. This touches me, feels infinitely generous. Daniel is the one who is really Michel's heir.

Daniel is also organizing the conclusive trip to the cemetery. He'll be in the same car as Hervé and François Ewald, Michel's assistant at the Collège de France, but he has assigned me to another, with Thierry. Almost immediately I'm bothered by it. I'd be in good company going to the burial with Daniel and Hervé, of course, but it shatters me like a punishment to have to go with Thierry, whom I hardly see any more, as well as an unknown driver who's also the one who was indiscreet enough to pass on the information about Michel's death, which Daniel had deemed it his duty to announce to him when it occurred. The man had told someone in charge at my newspaper, who'd then called me to express his surprise at not having gotten the information from me. I decide not to go, but it tugs at my conscience. I write a letter for Daniel, but it's almost too late for it to reach him. Hélie suggests his bringing it to him at the other end of Paris, since Daniel is near rue de Vaugirard, and I accept with overstated gratitude. I hope Daniel won't take it too badly. Hélie returns, informing me that he ran into him in the lobby of his building and gave him the letter while explaining what it was about. Daniel attached no bad importance to my opting out. Of course there's no reason for me to come if it's getting me down.

Libération prepares an issue of tributes for the day of the funeral. A female historian Michel respected comes to hand in her article. I can't remember whether she's aware that I knew him, and she says to me, "It's harsh, isn't it?" without adding anything else, and to me the word seems appropriate. For the newspaper Hervé sends me a text Michel had told him about in which he describes his deep love for Daniel. Publishing it is a way to please Daniel, and pleasing Daniel is the most we can do now for Michel. The text appears.

The funeral takes place early at the mortuary, an inherently grim place. Gérard and Hélie stop by my place to pick me up and take me there. I've accepted that favor with gratitude that I would have never dared express. This death is a disaster for everybody, and it's generous to grant me this special treatment. It's really crowded. My father appears and without a word throws his arms around me. I think that's the only time he ever did that. Gérard sees several people I don't know who know him because they were seeing Michel when Thierry lived on rue de Vaugirard and was already spending his days there. I'm afraid of being swallowed up by the crush, but Daniel spots us and brings us to our close friends. A friend from Michel's youth is there, handkerchief in hand, weeping in great sobs. The sight of it irritates me since I'm not crying and not even is Daniel. I find it soothing to have seen Michel again long after having seen him in such bad shape from the acid. Everything goes by quickly. Next, for a smaller audience, Gilles Deleuze, Michel's friend regained, says a few words that move me deeply. Then we separate. Hervé, Daniel and Thierry go back to their cars, and I leave with Gérard and Hélie. It's over.

Michel's very aged teacher, struck by my suffering at the funeral, wants to see me. Daniel tells me about it and gives me his phone number. I call and go over there. He's very kind, makes every effort to console me. I see him again. Having passed the age of eighty, he talks about Michel's luck in dying while still young, the fact that he took advantage of life and spared himself old age. He speaks to me about love. Sexuality is no longer his occupation or his preoccupation, of course, but he'd like me to kiss him. I comply, and it hardly bothers me at all. My body is rudderless as well, quite obviously.

I have dinner with Hervé who tells me that one of his friends has just broken her arm, the poor girl. He talks about it in such an appropriate tone that it flings me into a fit of laughter because how can I believe that it's affecting him? What kind of calamity is a broken arm? And he too is swept up into my wild laughter, making it our best moment since Michel's death.

My role as an efficient comforter during Michel's hospitalization, spurting out optimistic hypotheses not characteristic of Hervé's talents, undergoes a reversal starting with Michel's unexpected death. While I try not to collapse, Hervé rallies round Daniel, even inviting him to the island of Elba to that retreat he loves so much, which is a kind of magic place for him, his own rue de Vaugirard. Meanwhile, I go under, can't understand a thing. I'd finally seen the end of my infinitely calamitous adolescence and had started to take life head on, become aware that human beings shared the same planet, which had therefore seemed accessible to some degree. To put it simply, I'd realized happiness was possible. And now, suddenly, this discovery has become out of date, valueless. From this point forward I'll need to hope for less from existence. I thought I'd gained access to something eternal, and what seemed eternal has slipped away. What I thought was life was youth.

THEM

1

For the twenty-year anniversary of the death of Michel, *Libéra-tion* published a special supplement containing a long conversation with Daniel. In it he explained how the circum-stances of Michel's death, the way the two of them had been treated in the hospital, during which Daniel himself had been separated from contact with Michel while he was ill, had resulted in Daniel creating AIDES, the first French organiza-tion to help those stricken by AIDS. One doctor had talked him out of thinking that Michel was infected with the disease by claiming that if this were the case, he would have examined Daniel as well. Daniel made it clear that Michel himself hadn't disclosed he was infected with HIV, so it hadn't been up to Daniel to take on that task. "I had a problem to resolve: not speaking for him but also not doing nothing." I myself would adore finding a way to act, to write about the same thing, considering how long I've been wanting to speak about the rue de Vaugirard.

In the interview, Daniel also made the point that Michel hadn't been able to see whom he wanted to in the hospital, including Gilles Deleuze, Georges Canguilhem, and me. I phoned him to thank him for including me in this prestigious list but also maintained that it wasn't true, that of course I'd seen

Michel in the hospital. "I know you did" he answered, "but I really wanted you to appear in these pages."

Long before, after having written about Hervé's work, I'd discussed it with Michel, mentioning all the liberties Hervé took in his texts with facts that I myself had witnessed, and Michel answered, "Nothing happens to him but things that aren't true." I liked that remark so much I repeated it to Hervé, who quoted it in *To the Friend Who Did Not Save My Life* (*À l'ami qui ne m'a pas sauvé la vie*) but attributed it to Daniel. Since it appeared on a page in which everything he described was inexact compared to what he'd told me when the events happened, I at first believed he'd made the remark on purpose, as a way to twist the sentence full circle. No, he claimed, which left me a bit vexed for being expelled without reason from the relationship among the three of us—Michel, him and me. It was as if the untrue things were contaminating the true things, allowing literature to take over a truth that as a result was no longer one, had become fictitious only to remain real.

One day Michel had expressed his amusement about my relationship to the truth. I was telling him that Thierry would lie, and since he didn't think the word seemed appropriate, I explained. For example, when the two of us were traveling in Australia, where I'd gone to visit him while he was taking a break from his world tour, he'd claimed there was more than enough gasoline until the next stop, which was a complete lie, and we'd have run out of gas in open country—in the middle of the bush—if we hadn't miraculously found a gas station halfway there. Michel wasn't convinced by this example. It became quite clear to me that my relationship to truth also reflected my anxiety about the great open expanses of Australia and Thierry's superior resilience. If I myself had been in a position to exaggerate, I would have steered my answer in the opposite direction, claiming that we couldn't hold out more than a few miles at most; and obviously, if I were accused of lying, I would have denied it with all my heart. But I myself am more likely to say "I lied" rather than "I was wrong"; "Can I steal this pencil from you for a minute?" rather than, "Can I borrow it?"; because that's how I toy with language, just as my teenage brother would talk about having to "eat the medicine," which is what everybody does but nobody puts that way. I enjoy seeing speech imbued with a bit of imperfection and bluntness, because no matter the situation, no matter how gentle, bluntness and imperfection are always its most apt description. The entire universe is nothing more than a euphemism.

Never would I have been able to answer the way Daniel did, which I admired. Never could anyone in my family, I thought, twist a truth to reach another one. Whenever an author of a different publishing house sent my father a book, he'd make sure either to thank the person before having read it or to answer using a sentence with a double meaning ("I hope your novel will have the success it deserves"), which simultaneously allowed him to be polite and to be honest. This impressed me for years and years, until I myself was working for a newspaper and it was my turn to receive novels by authors whom I more or less knew, making the idea of writing books more concrete. For me this turned a courtesy into a discourtesy that conceived of books as products like any other you thank someone for, as if you'd been mailed a box of chocolates. One fine day, I started responding to what they were sending me by expressing the joy I took in reading these texts and offered my compliments. I got over this quickly. Fifteen days after I'd decided on this new strategy, on the street I ran into one of the authors, who thanked me in turn for my letter as a way of starting a conversation about his book that I actually hadn't read. I couldn't even remember the title, and getting out of the interaction without ruffling feathers became a major nuisance. So I abandoned my irresolute impulses for high-toned courtesy and returned ingloriously to honesty.

I may have been the grandson of a prosecutor, but my father was his son, and what was left of the adolescent in me found a new way to compete in terms of ethics. While reading Racine's biography by his son, I'd been struck by the episode in which Racine argues with Boileau and each writer holds firm to his own opinion, until Boileau asks Racine if he was intending to upset him, and the author of *Andromaque* answers, assuredly not. "Then you're wrong," says Boileau, "because you have." All the same, my father attached considerable importance to being right, which his professional success only reinforced (since he'd been right against everyone to publish such rejected or spurned authors); and yet, I believed such success didn't take sufficient account of the possibility of being wrong. When Pierre Bourdieu and he were angry at each other, my father gave me his own version of the conflict several times. Someone else had described it to me as an old couple going through a break-up, using the pretext of rationality to mask a more general and less controllable motive: "They can't stand each other any more." However, without fail, my father's explanation would include Bourdieu's exasperated accusation, which went, "Of course, you're always right." And, as if this single stand were all he had available, my father would characterize the remark as the bullet Bourdieu had used to shoot himself in the foot. He wasn't supposed to be duped, but he reckoned I might be. Such an obsession was also part of family life. He obviously held to a proverb I've never encountered "in French in the text," just in Tolstoy's novels: "Who excuses himself accuses himself." He never excused himself; but if he did, there was nothing to it, due to a sort of ostentatious high-mindedness. Not a question of power or virility—just honesty. Because he was right. And meanwhile, the contents of his editorial catalogue were all the proof he required that he knew how to turn his sensitivity into a clever compliment of his intelligence.

What pleased me so much in Daniel's lie was its simplicity, the fact that he was right to tell it because it was a better way to speak a truth without harming anything or anyone than another unimportant truth would be.

Given the vicissitudes of the press, the special report had appeared a bit in advance, and I called Daniel again on the anniversary of Michel's death. He didn't sound well on the phone, and I advised him to have a doctor come over. A bit worried, I phoned again the next day for news, insisting on the doctor and offering to stop by a little later. When I arrived, the doctor had just left, and it turned out that Daniel had needed one. Now everything was going better, but it had been a close call. This wasn't the first time since Michel had died that I'd returned to rue de Vaugirard. However, my visits had become rare and didn't leave any impressions on me. When I think of the apartment again, I always see it the way Michel had furnished it when I lived there. On the pillar where three photos of Daniel used to be, there were now three of Michel arranged the same way, redolent of the same kind of happy spirits. The rest of the space, I was definitely aware, had been organized differently, but the old way was still imprinted on my mind. The current reality had none of the intensity of the old one. It needs to be kept in mind that I'll stop at nothing to make Michel survive. It had been my home and no longer was. Even so, anything concerning Michel still gives me the impression that this is my place. While he was alive, the feeling of being home grew stronger and stronger. Obviously, he's the link between Daniel and me. The two of us never spent an evening alone together while Michel was alive and doubtlessly never wanted to. Now we're always happy to see each other, because we know we can talk about Michel with full knowledge of the facts, because of how lucky we were to know him, and his affection for us and ours for him has become our chief mainstay, a privilege we can always draw upon after that sad August 4 night when he died for us.

One of the things in my life I'm proudest of is my friendship with Michel. Each time I fall in love, when I'm filled with the potential for generosity, I suffer from this lack: I can't offer a visit with Michel. More than fifteen years after his death, when I announced to my father that I had just formed a domestic partnership with Rachid, he answered in a kind voice that he was happy for me but added nothing to that and didn't suggest meeting him. Maybe it was up to me to offer. But he didn't ask any questions. I obviously didn't really want to present him to my father, either, since I didn't insist. In any case, I knew it would be complicated, because the family restricted my father's open-mindedness. Not many view meeting their in-laws or their son-in-law as something to hope for. That was also the case for Rachid.

After Hervé's death, which happened long after Michel's because research on the disease had progressed, I gave in to my doctor who'd wanted me to take an HIV test. Up until then, I'd contented myself with acting in a way that would keep me from infecting anyone if I was or from getting infected if I wasn't. The anxiety inherent in waiting for results was increased by the fact that I didn't know anyone who'd had this test and turned out to be negative. I was the first. When I told Bernardo, who had every reason to be interested, he said I should repeat it to my parents, who had to be worried. It was something I hadn't thought of. Nor had anything about their conduct led me to think so. I phoned my father, and he didn't respond at all. His silence bothered me as much as my declaration must have bothered him. We never spoke about it again. My parents knew what Michel and Hervé had died of and were aware of my intimacy with them. They could have easily thought no sex was involved, but there was nothing that allowed them to be sure of it. Worry was so familiar to them (as a teenager I'd been struck by the dedication Robbe-Grillet had written them for *La Jalousie* in which he raised them to the status of "wonderful partners in anxiety"), and they truly were such wonderful transmitters of that emotion that they didn't want to hear any talk about it. Because I belonged to the family, they obviously had no unwholesome interest in the situation, given that exaggerated closeness at the heart of the family that surrounds filiation. All they felt was a wholesome lack of interest, as if they were repressing the idea of fatality and including it with illness, homosexuality and anxiety itself in the same *terra* they wanted to keep *incognita* as long as possible.

My father, who avidly studied Hebrew culture in his youth, claimed to me on two occasions during my youth that the divine curse had to be interpreted in the opposite sense of how it usually was. When a man is cursed "at the third generation" (and not "until the third," he made clear), it is much more severe than it is at the seventh. Because the meaning, according to what he told me, is that that man's lineage will end either at the third or the seventh generation, and such is the substance of the curse. In a novel I invented a writer whose most important text begins with the sentence, "Make children so you won't have to choose whom to love," and I actually do think that this is a motive for accumulating generations. By having children, my father, who liked to control everything, fell smack dab into a situation that couldn't be controlled. Choosing was his profession, his pride, his power and his life. But you don't choose your children. Certain circumstances rendered him cursed at the second generation according to his system of calculation. His only grandchildren were the children of my brother, who didn't want him to see them. He talked to me about it again on a day we had lunch near Les éditions de Minuit. I was telling him that the more he hurried things, the more it made my brother dig in his heels, that all he had to do was wait for the children to grow up and decide on their own to meet him or not; and the expression on his face combined with a gesture of his arm demonstrated how unreliable he found such a perspective. I hadn't yet understood that for him time was an enemy. Michel had died of AIDS, Hervé had died of AIDS, as well as Hélie and many other friends and lovers in my circle. I'd forgotten that it wasn't the only cause of mortality, even though a fall from the eighth floor had killed Valentin. For me, my father was dramatizing things, a practice that might have been common for him in his professional life but wasn't usual in his private one.

At the death of my grandfather, a month after he had celebrated his ninetieth birthday with all his children, grandchildren and great-grandchildren, my father had told me that a happy life was reaching that age without having seen any of your descendants die. Long before, during the period when his father was in good health and my father must have still felt more or less competitive toward him, he'd told me about a legal case that had caused quite a stir. Although my grandfather had been the prosecutor, he'd called for the acquittal of a woman who'd killed her husband, a prominent citizen who was humiliating and physically abusing her. We grandchildren thought of our grandfather as an intractable prosecutor, because he had demanded and obtained more death penalties for collaborators than any district attorney, and in this case, he made himself conspicuous by his leniency. My father belittled what he had done by telling me that my grandfather had only acted out of respect for the family, as if that notion were totally foreign to him and he didn't recognize the same kind of thing in himself. Michel discussed that story by taking the opposite tack, putting my grandfather's courage at the forefront with that familiar though infrequent pout he had (his lower lip stuck out) when giving an admiring account of behavior that impressed him.

My father died when he was fifteen years younger than his own father, without having seen any of his descendants die, but also without having seen either of his children stop living alone. Unlike him, his parents were fond of lots of get-togethers that he always went to, supposedly reluctantly, including that ninetieth birthday party for my grandfather when I got lost in the subway and had to arrive late. I could read the relief of my father's face when I finally reached the apartment and hadn't missed the celebration. My father always favored my coming for lunch rather than for dinner so he could plan to take advantage of my presence and still go to bed at his usual time; and there were never any get-togethers with the children at my parents' home. Had he acted otherwise, different bonds might have been forged, and my father might have gotten to know his grandchildren. He loved the family but not family life. As for Michel's family, I only met a nephew one time on rue de Vaugirard. At Michel's death, I'd hear about the brother who took things in hand and made the trip from the hospital to Vendeuvre to inform their mother. His father had been a prominent provincial doctor, and to me Michel's family seemed a little like Flaubert's. For my father, things hadn't turned out as planned, and this had something to do with me. Something fraudulent happened to him: his family, his descendants.

Homosexuality transformed the rules. Intimacy changed camps. This prevented family solidarity in the strictest sense— from my ancestors to my descendants. Seen from that perspective, the only child between my parents and me remained me. As a result, the affection between us endured, but intimacy took on a lurid cast, stranded as it was somewhere between childhood and sexuality, having lost contact with reality, making it less legitimate than the things happening to Hervé. It was restricted to and at the same time enlarged by my family of friends, that fictitious family that became the real one, as if a long quest had finally led me to my biological peers. And no curse of that order ever struck down such intimacy. It was transmitted across generations so effectively that both Daniel and I inherited our relationship from Michel.

2

I never bothered Michel. I did, of course, but he was careful to
keep it from seeming so. Right until the end, when he was going
to die and cared more than anything else about putting the
finishing touches to his books, he'd answer when I phoned and
never put off or cut short our conversation. Sometimes, that
made me resent my father, who didn't share those scruples. When
I'd call him at the publishing house, almost as a matter of course
I had the feeling of stealing time from him, and not only from
him. I felt as if I were interrupting him in the midst of decisions
involving the future of the world, or at least the literary one. His
perpetual withdrawal masked either his fear or my awkwardness
about the potential problem of too intimate a conversation
between us. After all, affection often takes the place of intimacy
in family relationships.

When Hervé was dying, it was similar. I left it up to him to
call most of the time, to choose the moments; but whenever I
myself did, I was always welcome. (When I moved a few months
before his death, just in time for him still to be able to climb to
the sixth floor without an elevator, he told me after a summary
inspection that he was happy to know I was living in such a
pleasant place, a generous thought that for me seemed to come
from another age. I'd have to grow older to know how to possess

it.) From this point of view as for certain others, Hervé may have remained my generational peer, but he acquired a maturity that outdid mine to such an immeasurable extent that it was a bit like the mother in *Remembrance of Things Past* (*À la recherché du temps perdu*) who becomes the grandmother for the narrator after the death of his real grandmother. For me, there was something of Michel in Hervé.

That, however, required some time. When Michel died, there was still no question of Hervé passing away. "I'm going to die" is the most banal declaration in the world, something anyone at all could state at any moment at all, and without fail it's imbued with a dramatic character. Its temporal imprecision mysteriously implies a fatal immediacy. The hero of a detective film or Jack Bauer in *24* saying it takes me back to Hervé, who never said it. It's a violent French occurrence of the English present progressive.[1] *As he lay dying*. In that Faulknerian permutation that is a vision of Hervé,[2] I identify mysteriously with the word *as*, the one who's not about to die and who says goodbye even so, and who obviously will also die. The phrase that the Duke de Guermantes says to a dying Swann in order not to spoil the party for himself, his "You'll bury us all," a remark of doubtful taste that Proust blows up out of proportion, is in a certain sense only a synonym for *as*. (*As we're surviving*). Death is the great disruption.

Hervé and I were angry at each other for a short time a year after Michel's death. Why? Because he kept bothering me. I was writing a novel motivated by my bereavement and was in the grip of an

---

1. Translator's note: The "violent French occurrence of the English present progressive" to which the author is referring is *Je vais mourir* ("I am going to die.") Progressive tenses in French are rarer than they are in English.
2. Translator's note: A reference to Faulkner's novel, complicated here by the fact that for his purpose the author has temporarily transformed the French title of the book (*Tandis que j'agonise*; "*As I Lay Dying*") into *Tandis qu'il agonise* ("*As He Lay Dying*").

emotion that was doing me good. Michel's death had led to my taking heroin more often, and I was using junk to write this book, which was, on the other hand, an attempt to describe the effects of acid. I had invented the requirement that every session with H had to be integral to my making progress with my novel, and Hervé was calling me routinely while I was deep in my work. There was no doubt of my having made him understand this the times before; and one day he took it more harshly and told me to go to the devil. Not realizing the nearly permanent irritation the heroin itself was causing, I was surprised that such a simple occurrence had led to such a reaction, but I wasn't worried since I was certain of our friendship. I would call him back when the time was right, after my novel was no longer coming between us (when it was finished, it became Hervé's favorite of the books I'd written). There was another thing that kept me from believing a lasting breach was possible, and I knew it was the same for him: it was Michel who had instigated our relationship, and never would we have dared to fall out permanently if he were still alive; nor could it be a question of us taking advantage of his death to feed our anger. It would have been shameful from every point of view. We reconciled rapidly after having met accidentally in the street, even if the agency for it came in the form of a dinner to which we had both arrived in advance and been seated in different parts of the restaurant where we couldn't see each other, making each of us believe that the other hadn't come until I got up to go to the men's room and finally spotted Hervé. He had figured I was taking my revenge by being late, something that I, because of a long family tradition that includes my father and grandfather, never am.

A few years later, we spent two years together in Rome at the villa Medici. The idea had come from Hervé, who had been awarded a residency of two years the first time he took part in the competition, although I failed to obtain it for the same length of time until the following year (he spent a third year there by accompanying me when he was no longer a resident). I arrived in Rome with all of the Austrian writer Thomas Bernhard's books that had been translated so far. I'd only discovered him a few months before, and because they fascinated me, I was thinking of writing about him and needed to have all his books accessible. Hervé lacked my enthusiasm for getting down to work and began by borrowing a book from me, then returned it to take another and so on, until he as well had read almost everything by Bernhard, whom he laughingly critiqued in a way that contradicted his eagerness to devour them. A few months later, he told me he wanted me to read a manuscript. Such readings were a significant aspect of our relationship. He was always eager for my reactions to his work, but this time there was an extra anxiety. I rapidly read through his novel, which was not yet called *To the Friend Who Did Not Save My Life* and which Hervé had temporarily entitled *Pends-toi Bill!*,[3] one of the last sentences of the book, as a way of overplaying the aggressive character and using irony to counteract some of the seriousness.

I loved the text and that made him happy. But his anxiety wouldn't have been as intense if it had only been literary. He was afraid I'd find fault—since I was rather expert at doing so—from a more or less moral perspective, because he'd made Michel a character. And yet that was precisely one of the elements in the book that really bowled me over—it was really he. Hervé wondered if I hadn't also noticed something else. Since I swore by Thomas Bernhard, he was worried I'd find his appropriation of Bernhard's style ridiculous. I was laying claim to being an expert about that as well, without even having identified the TB bacterium that was a part of those pages. It was the occasion for an exceptionally merry evening.

---

3. Translator's note: "Go fuck yourself, Bill!" or, more literally, "Go hang yourself, Bill!"

Hervé had always also expected a commercial literary success, and he was expected to have a bestseller published in his lifetime. This text was sure to be the best one for it. He wanted to go for broke. He'd had a row with my father and left Les éditions de Minuit without anyone attempting to make me party to their dispute. This time he wanted me to submit the manuscript to my father, because they were no longer speaking. I accepted without any reluctance and was content to be the go-between through which a text like that would be brought to Minuit.

When I saw my father again, after he'd read what was now called *To the Friend Who Did Not Save My Life*, he began remarking without much affect about the state of the manuscript, how it was full of spelling errors as crude as they were numerous. That annoyed me. I had read the same pages without having been struck by them, carried away as I'd been by my passionate reading. Mainly, focusing on such a detail almost seemed like bad taste when compared to the book's power. My response was rather curt, and my father obviously took this as understandable in the face of an announcement that was about to amount to a rejection. Then I reached the point of explaining myself more clearly, voicing my astonishment that circumflex accents (since the imperfect subjunctive produced a trove of errors in the manuscript) had acquired an importance so much more significant than Hervé's death. "Hervé's death?" said my father. He was surprised, close to losing his composure. It was the only time in his life, I would swear, when he suggested a fresh reading without any prompting.

In fact, since the narrator says in the first sentence of the text that he thinks he became infected with AIDS three months ago, my father hadn't gone any farther biographically. He hadn't imagined Hervé was ill. That seemed crazy to me, as well as a bad sign, because a second reading wasn't going to clarify anything the first hadn't. At the same time, I was fascinated. Anyone at all who read this book would have felt the impending death of the author—even a tenth-rate reader would be competent enough to sense that. And yet it had escaped my father, precisely because he was an exceptional reader. He was so entrenched in literature that to appreciate it he had no need for factual links with reality, for anything at all explicitly biographical, because not only could he disregard such a thing but even had trouble doing otherwise. This also shed light on the relationship between him and me. And what about myself? Would I as well have escaped being captured by such a reading if I hadn't been so close to Hervé?

The next day, after finishing his second reading, my father reiterated his rejection of the book. My Spanish publisher, who translated my first novels, told me about a drawing by Saul Steinberg he kept on the wall of his office. It showed an editor speaking to an author. As is often the case with Steinberg, the layout of the words he was saying formed other words. In this case, all the editor's explanations and compliments were arranged to form one word: "NO." I never knew whether the financial or theoretical reasons my father gave in such a situation had any value at all, whether he was taking advantage of the situation to voice a problem he held close to his heart, assured as he was of a captive audience; or whether he was behaving the way he did to uphold the self-esteem of the person he was speaking to, since it would have been worse to say he didn't want his text simply because he didn't like it. For *To the Friend Who Did Not Save My Life*, he placed moral reasons in the foreground—the memory of Michel Foucault. That offended me for two reasons. On the one hand, I didn't see how that memory was being attacked in the slightest sense by Hervé's text, who in my eyes was, on the contrary, accomplishing the feat of restoring Michel as he really was, and describing how he really was amounted to the greatest tribute you could offer. On the other, I found it shockingly inappropriate to place anyone at all, aside from maybe Daniel, above Hervé as the guarantor of Michel's memory. I interpreted all critique carried out from this point of view as usurpation. But I took note of my father's words and reported them to Hervé, who found another, better arrangement.

My father's refusal hadn't been across the board. He told me he couldn't assure the success of the book, had decided not to obtain it through any channel that in any way existed outside the sphere of literature; but he gave his word to publish it if no other press would. For him that was a familiar declaration, because one kind of thing in his profession that excited him was a power struggle. Those authors who took it into their heads to give into them would find themselves bound hand and foot (something that never happened, since once my father had accrued enough advance conditions to assure victory and eliminate the need for rearguard battle strategies, he'd lose all interest). Specifically, such a possibility was unlikely. Of course Hervé would easily find another publisher for *To the Friend Who Did Not Save My Life*. It annoyed me that my father presented as a generosity what I saw as an abuse of power. But one of his strengths at this point in his life was being attached to his professional role and never deviating from it willingly. It went so far as his angrily rescinding the possibility of any conversation expressing affinity if I called to speak about literature. In those cases you were fiddling with a moral absolute. I remember how stupefied he was recounting that during one of his regular visits with Beckett, he'd offered to relieve Sam of all the manuscripts he was getting and that must have been cluttering up his normally sparse apartment. "'No need,' Sam answered," he told me. "'I throw them in the trash.'" It was something my father, who venerated him, could never get over. All in all, my father was devoid of a radical method to keep from being bothered—constantly and neurotically afraid of such an affliction.

A few months after Michel's death, *Libération* sent me to interview Simone Signoret, who had just published some writing. I'd read her book because Michel had been close to her. He spoke of her often affectionately, and he saw her a great deal while Thierry was living with him. I myself had never met her and now wanted to—through a kind of transitivity of relationships, feeling as I did interposed between those two friends. Maybe that was why I'd enjoyed her book. Signoret was going to die that year and was now almost blind, wearing a pair of dark glasses. Full of emotion at the end of the interview, I guided her back from the café to her home. As we slowly walked across the square, a kindly looking young man approached, ready with notebook and pen. With the politest voice in the world, in a strong foreign accent and delivering his words at a snail's pace, he asked, "Please, Madame, would it suit you to give me your autograph?" He gently placed the notebook in one hand and the pen in the other, as she smilingly answered, "It suits me completely." And her friendship with Michel suddenly showed forth in all its evidence. I'd also like to think that, in the end, the success of *To the Friend Who Did Not Save My Life* at Gallimard suited my father completely.

3

In her book *Monsieur Proust* Céleste Albaret recounts her experiences as a young housekeeper for the great writer and says that the author of *Remembrance of Things Past* helped her long after his death. When potential employers understood whom they were dealing with, they rushed to her. When I first read this text, I had no idea that I'd meet Michel someday, but I explicitly understood that I as well would have felt a special brand of kindness for her and that doing something for her would have seemed like doing it for Proust. For the writers whose texts I love, I feel gratitude on the personal level that it would be wonderful to be able to express.

While Michel was alive, I had always been discreet about my relationship with him, divulging it only to those with whom I was intimate. It was almost a perversion; when someone was saying bad things about him, my greatest vengeance was to let that person keep talking in the hope that someday, in my absence, without any possibility of making up for it, that person would learn about having chosen the wrong recipient for those cruel words. For an instant after Michel died, I'd have wanted the entire world to know about our closeness. Death wasn't very familiar to me back then. Having known him was all that remained of Michel. I was an anonymous Céleste who habitually attracted no one. I also had no ambition for a career in a household staff. Our fates may have been different, but in my crippled sentimental education my intimacy with Michel suddenly became the best thing I had. Any kind of help would have been good for me. And little by little, that help came from having known him, without any need to tell any unconcerned members of the population about it. It helps me that others are familiar with him, even if they were born after his death and enjoy no other intimacy then the pleasant task of reading him—I feel capable of giving them the same kindness that Céleste received, but in a disproportionate fashion. They don't know it, but they are my imaginary brothers.

A year after Michel's death, Hervé asked me for a text on friendship for *L'Autre Journal*, a weekly he now worked for. I wrote a few lines peppered with references to Michel and rue de Vaugirard, as well as about Hervé and his work, comingling our relationships (hadn't his death transformed all my connections?). Today I'm grateful to Michel for making them seem casual.

> He had left me his keys so I could take care of his banana tree while he was away (he used to flambé some of its fruits and serve them as dessert at the dinners he gave at his place). I took the keys but I forgot to water the tree, I only clumsily burned his Joan of Arc engraving (but wasn't she destined for that?) and changed the arrangement of his library by replacing all the books I'd paged through anywhere at all. I was aware how attached he was to that print and his banana tree, which was dead, and I was full of remorse and fear as I waited for him to return. He came back in a very merry mood; his trip had gone wonderfully (he'd travelled through Africa, almost married an attractive Kenyan and swam next to a crocodile in the Gambia River). Discovering the disaster at home, he'd merely advised

me, "You have to take things philosophically." Philosophy is also a very friendly practice.

I had forgotten all about this text. It's Bernardo who reminds me of it when I'm talking to him about the book I want to do. He had read it before getting to know me and thinks that its tone, which has stayed in his memory all these years, may be the voice I ought to adopt. But I've just finished a novel in a completely different voice that I undertook to get out of the depressive slump in which Michel's death had left me. This tragedy isn't my explicit subject, but it was on my mind during the entire writing process, my way of acclimating to it, of recovering the sweetness of my friendship with Michel. In my own way, I'm conjuring Michel and the last acid trip, but especially Gérard, especially the Vaugirard years, which have already been branded as an entity and already represent a divide, a sealed period in my life. They aren't limited to him, but he personified them. My bonds with Hervé and Gérard occur in the present time, but they wouldn't have been the same if Michel had taught me nothing. He perfected my affections.

Hervé and I have the habit of choosing the other as first reader, when each manuscript is completed. For the first time, chance leads to a dinner one evening when we are planning to exchange manuscripts, since both of us have finished at the same time. One of our never-ending jokes is pretending we're afraid of losing each other's manuscript, that it might get stolen, or that one of us might drop it into the Seine. In his book *Jérôme Lindon*, Jean Echenoz recounts that, one day when he was experiencing that type of fear, my father joked, "So a lot of your manuscripts have been stolen, in the métro?" (In fact, one of my father's favorite stories was about coming close to scattering the pages of *Molloy*, Samuel Becket's first text, in the métro, after he'd been seized by a fit of giggles with the manuscript in his hands.)

A few years earlier, Michel had given me a book for which he'd written the preface, and I accidentally left it on rue de Vaugirard, giving him the great pleasure of mocking the profound disinterest I must have felt for his work and pretending to be afraid that this might be justified. But Hervé doesn't lose my manuscript nor I his. I devour his. The next day, each of us has read the other's book with enthusiasm and each of us is claiming the other's is the better one.

Hervé's text *My Parents* (*Mes parents*) is a dementedly and delightfully violent take on a theme so universal that it would even fascinate those born as orphans or even given away at birth by their mothers. And even me, then. My cruel interpretation of the characters who contribute to the book's appeal is based on the fact that I strongly suspect they're based on Hervé's parents. However, like my father, my relationship to literature is filtered so confidently through fiction that I also have no problem seeing them merely as ink-and-paper entities that don't exist in the real world and are therefore out of reach of any compassion since it as well can only be fictitious. When the book is being published and Hervé wants a red band placed around the cover reading, "Tender is hate," I loudly proclaim this as a betrayal, recouping the violence of his text by means of psychology and a large-scale offensive. Why not print "So there!" on the band, which would be more honest, I'll suggest. I'm all the more at ease about championing this settling of counts since I myself have never done so explicitly. And because, when Hervé was working with Patrice Chéreau on the screenplay for *The Wounded Man* (*L'Homme blessé*), he had me read a version of it, as if we were equally competent in both literature and film, and there was so little truth to that that I hadn't known what to say except, "I'd take out the family," which is about as sensible a piece of advice as suggesting cutting out the landing from *The Longest Day*.

The family in *The Wounded Man* resembled the one in *Mes parents*. For me Hervé's parents were just his creatures—what he wrote about or told amusing tales about during our evenings. I was only in contact with them—if you can call it that—once while he was alive. He was going to die very soon and obsessively worried that whatever money he now had from his successes would revert to his parents. He had married with a special contract he hoped would deprive them of it and nevertheless wasn't completely reassured. If his parents contested the will after he died, he wanted one of his friends armed with a letter to go to court to express his distinct wish clearly: everything was to go to Christine, his wife, and the children she'd had with Hervé's lover, and nada for mommy and daddy. He asked me to help him draw up the letter by writing a rough draft. I did this with great enthusiasm, as if it were a refreshing exercise in insidiousness. I kept in mind what would be most useful and convincing in the context of a potential legal suit and had a field day, despite how cautious I am with my own family. After all, Hervé's parents weren't flesh and blood for me but his creation and a way for me to show my solidarity, just as fans support a team by booing and insulting the opposite team in the guise of encouraging theirs. Hervé was thrilled with my letter, to my embarrassed astonishment, and he recopied it on the spot just as it was, endowing it with illusory veracity, then gave it to me in case I needed to use it. I only saw his parents once, in Clamart where the funeral was held, because the burial, which I would skip just as I had Michel's, was to take place on the island of Elba; the father made the trip there with the hearse. I never looked at the corpse, a lesson I'd learned from Michel's death. In front of the coffin of their thirty-six-year-old son, Hervé's parents were real. They were truly father and mother.

Another relative was there as well. While all the people close to Hervé—except me—were waiting in Italy for the actual burial, I was given the responsibility of making sure his funeral wishes were respected in case his father or mother did anything counter to them. The prospect of having to exercise this power terrified me. There was no call for it, and there were no more incidents except for the will. But as I was standing there, a woman came toward me to offer me her condolences as "Hervé's friend," and to excuse her presence that she feared could be bothersome, she added that her son had just died of AIDS and that she just had the feeling that she should be there. I was paralyzed. I could only look at her for an instant, nicely, I hope, and was incapable of responding with a word, of offering the slightest help in the world. That moment's compulsion for inaction is what I regret more than anything else on that sinister morning at the very beginning of January. For a completely unknown woman, I felt the pity that Hervé had so well protected me from when it came to his parents.

Mine? This wasn't the day to think about it. I went to lunch at their place the following Saturday, and as I spoke of the ceremony and mentioned the retreat on the island of Elba where Hervé had wanted to be buried, understandably assuming that his death had extinguished any possibility of my father feeling animosity toward him, he answered my remark—which actually didn't have to be answered—by saying that he found it moving that the place where his corpse would lie had been chosen in such a way. When he himself died, and plans about where to bury him had to be made, I learned that at the exact period in which Hervé had died he'd found a burial plot at the cemetery of Montparnasse with probably enough room for us all, twenty steps from Beckett's tomb. After the matter had been completed, he'd said, "That way we won't be far from Sam." And that was especially moving for me since in my place it would have been unseemly to go and get buried in the provincial cemetery near Michel's birthplace. By what right? On what grounds—seeing that I didn't even want to be?

The day after that day we exchanged manuscripts, when Hervé is still unaware he is sick, he calls me to tell me how much he likes my book, and that approval is particularly meaningful seeing that he'd noticed everything in the text connected to Michel. Maybe in the end he would have preferred the text I give him next for *L'Autre Journal* to be in the same voice. Although my relations—even literary—with my father have settled down, I don't give him the book in manuscript, contenting myself with waiting for it to be published. He calls me as soon as he has read it to thank me and offer his congratulations, adding with satisfaction, "This is proof that you're someone good." I gladly accept the compliment, amused that, aside from the accuracy of the remark, my father needed a novel to come to such a realization. That's just like him—and just like me.

A few weeks after the publication of the book, I receive a fantastic letter from a young Brazilian named Bernardo, whom I meet and will end up spending years with. One day, after we've become truly intimate, I tell him about rue de Vaugirard. By coincidence he knows the apartment—or rather, the studio. Daniel is loaning it to a Brazilian university student who's a friend of Bernardo, and he's already visited him there. I bring up Michel himself. As proof of my high level of trust, I prepare to tell him about that last acid trip. He stops me, because he also knows that story. It has been shared with such a small number of people that I can't get over it. It turns out that a close friend of Bernardo has had an adventure with Monsieur Marc from whom she obtained the information, sharing it with Bernardo. Bernardo knew the entire story apart from the fact that I was part of it. Starting with Michel, I begin writing, and the published book brings me back to this in another way. His intimacy runs through a small circle: two years after his death, he's still there, concretely and fully in the actuality of my life.

At rue de Vaugirard I was the boy of the house, like Caroline in the story by Willa Cather, the girl in Croisset at the home of her uncle, who was writing *Madame Bovary*; and I was Céleste Albaret, the woman in the apartment lined with cork with someone who was dying and taking ages not to finish *Remembrance of Things Past*. At the same time, there's no relationship. I didn't share daily life with Michel, have hardly any correspondence to publish and, unlike Céleste, didn't appear in the work. The dedications for Michel's last books that I can be faulted for his never writing for me definitely would have helped me, and I trust him enough to know that they would have been convincing. To demonstrate how much he liked my novel, whose point of departure was Michel's death, Hervé claimed to me that any friend should offer such a thing to a friend and that any friend ought to take it upon himself to write a dedication for any friend at all. At times I'm troubled by sex, can't distinguish very well between love and friendship. I'm persuaded that everything in me that honors friendship is honoring Michel: isn't that love? I can't meet anyone without thinking of him. It's not that I imagine what he would have thought of this new friend; it's that I'm persuaded that our meeting wouldn't have been possible without him, would never have occurred. I don't underestimate my parents' contribution to the qualities I posses; but the pressure of a father (or mother)-son relationship is clearly a shackle, as if people are crushed by a sort of psychological structuralism.

Right after the death of Michel, I first saw only suffering. However, gradually I felt like Jean Valjean did after Bishop Myriel, filled with a responsibility for kindness (how I got over that is another story). Later, Michel obviously seemed like the friend who saved my life. I'd been the boy of the apartment, the one in farces who arrives just when the other one is leaving and leaves just when the other one is coming back. But when the other one has left for good, seeing that the farce has taken a turn for the worse, any way to return is kaput. Our fates were linked. And when they were unlinked, they still were. I would have wanted to keep squatting in at least an imaginary space, a rue de Vaugirard that became a world as submerged as Atlantis. It was my only hope, and heroin kept it alive. I was the young man of the apartment, but there was no longer any apartment nor youth. And yet, the apartment and youth would still be there to help me, throughout my life, like those consequences of Michel that never abandon me.

4

For family reasons, my father's death wasn't announced until after the funeral. There were very few of us at the cemetery, and we lunched with my mother, who afterward wanted to be alone. Rachid wasn't in France, and I'd told him not to return for it. Besides, he'd never met my father. Unlike my mother, I had no desire to be alone, and that afternoon I went to the paper, where I happened to have a column to do for the next day. For the time being, I had nothing to do, but being surrounded by people and activity is what I needed. To occupy my mind, I asked the person who sat next to me—who greeted me softly and would write the editorial column for *Libération*—about the news of the day, meaning, the opening pages including page one. "Your father," he answered. Five minutes later, another colleague came into the office and asked me the same question. "My father," I answered, slightly bothered that he'd spoken to me. "Why?" he asked. "Because he's dead," I said. "My condolences," he answered. "But then, what are you doing here?" And instead of telling him to go shove it, I offered a pathetic justification.

The next day, as I looked through the paper, moved by everything I read, I was struck by the fact that, counting Michel and Hervé, this was the third time in my life that the death of someone I loved had been announced on the front page of *Libération*.

Just as there had been a magnificent full-page photo of Michel bending in darkness over his desk, which was the only thing illuminated, this time there was one of my father standing in the street in front of the door to éditions de Minuit, looking as elegant, robust and smiling as he'd really been. I didn't know what to make of it, but it was something I noticed. It felt odd: every bereavement I experienced was a sort of public bereavement about which unknown people had to be informed. It mattered to me, since I had been struck by it. I devoured the pages on my father in a way I hadn't been able to do seventeen years earlier, when Michel had died, when I'd been incapable of seeing the event so abruptly officialized, even for a much greater number of people. As I had when Michel died, I saved these newspapers like books, if only because of the ephemeral nature of the press, which doesn't lend itself to republication. Saving them comes from devotion and an imperative more intense than those same feelings for books. I hid them away in a cupboard, to keep from rediscovering them by chance because I was acutely aware there would be moments when becoming absorbed in them again might be good but that there would be many others when I needed to protect myself from these photos and the mourning they occasioned. Consolation would be too strong a word, but at the time, something about reading them was related to a type of reassurance and it felt satisfying. These pages, synonyms of the importance of a fact that existed on a personal level for me, were proof of my luck. I had known those who merited tribute better than the people giving it had known them, and for years I myself had offered them homage while they were still living. I had done it my way, with all my affection and without waiting for such a grim occasion.

I never forgot the opening sentences of *The Great Gatsby*:

In my younger and more vulnerable years my father gave me some advice that I've been turning over in my mind ever since.

"Whenever you feel like criticizing any one," he told me, "just remember that all the people in this world haven't had the advantages that you've had."

My father never admonished me with such words. I don't know if they matched his beliefs because you'd have to be damned sure of yourself as a parent to say them, but what Fitzgerald wrote corroborates something implicit in the way I digested my education. The announcements of these deaths, sad as it was, hadn't cast a pall even for an entire day over most of these readers, who took them as news and could rely upon friends, lovers or children as if it what had happened were of little import; but I was lucky enough not to be like them. I had an immense and eternal advantage over them by being devastated by the information and its consequences. My despair itself was destined to bring me peace again, because I knew what I was losing, and I was losing it because I had had it.

The real shock, actually, was Michel's death. With age, death enters into the order of things, but at the time I hadn't aged enough. And time passing troubled me as much as it worked to soothe me. Although I missed Michel, I assumed millions of other people also missed him whether they knew it or not. His voice and intelligence could have stood up to a thousand attritions in this world. His death had taken me unawares because AIDS wasn't very familiar. The carnage was just beginning, and because the sick were declining so quickly there wasn't any way to prepare yourself for it. Hervé died at a much younger age but after a much slower process of dying, which gave him time to come to grips with some aspects of the illness and their effects. That was also the case for my father. I had gotten used to it over a period of a few weeks, which didn't diminish the torment but still lessened its brutality. And I was receiving loads of condolences. Even the paper presented me in print at the end of the main article as the deceased's son and colleague of the newspaper's editor, a company employee. It was nice of them, but it didn't touch me. In their eyes I had a right to it, and that was all.

As Daniel had asked me, I hadn't informed the paper when I'd learned that Michel had died, which my departmental head scolded me for when he learned about it himself. I'd benefited by our family's respectability when I announced my father's death after a delay to Agence France Presse. They'd already received the information and had surely written his obituary, but they'd thanked me for it. For Michel, everything had been done in haste, in that hustle and bustle of newspapers I adore, when an unexpected event arrives just at the close of that edition and everybody has to get down to a torturous deadline, helped as it is by how moved and filled with excitement they all are. That day, of course, I wasn't there, but subsequently I've often ended up being one of the journalists swept up by the professional urgency that colors the dailies. In fact, I actually wasn't aware of the day Michel had died since I'd just arrived at *Libération*. One day, I attended the burial of a colleague, a boy I liked a lot, but I was glad I wasn't the one lying there at the bottom of the hole. I had always found Père-Lachaise to be a wonderful place. It was good weather, appropriately calm for this kind of setting and ceremony; and at the very instant I began thinking that all in all this was a pleasant afternoon, I also told myself that I should never have thought that and that the next funeral I went to wouldn't feel so al fresco. And actually, my father's death turned out to be barely a few months later.

Likewise—although I don't mean chronologically—every major event arising in the cultural domain since I've worked at *Libération* has reawakened the same energy that Michel's death must have provoked. Each time I deliberately forget that for others my excitement is heartache and that I've shared their feeling more often than my turn. It's always strange to come back to the paper the next day and again find—if I may borrow the obit term used by the press—those who've "buried" Michel one day, those who've buried Hervé on another and those who've buried my father on yet another, and then have to start relating to them in the usual way, to all those who in their own way have served as specialists for the people I've loved and never stop cherishing. The next day, or the day after that for the most sensitive, my colleagues move on to other things; another death, possibly, like funereal intellectuals who knock off the job with the necessary talent and tact, with the emotion that gives the day its kick but ends with it, just as I, too, have done a hundred times.

I started at *Libération* less than three months before the death of Michel, who had soothed my anxieties about the perspective of a change by being enthusiastic about my transfer. He'd assisted at the birth of the newspaper, maintained a special relationship with it. When we were living on rue de Vaugirard, for the same reason we'd performed the deplorable act of devouring Daniel's diet cookies, convinced as we were that we had to take advantage of everything from day to day, we'd open the publications Michel subscribed to and, once read, would often even throw them away, until he told me he'd been making sure to save them all. My father was a *Le Monde* fanatic, and despite the fact that I was working at *Libération*, had no scruples about saying on those rare occasions when he had guests other than me at the house that he felt as if he were reading in my paper what he'd read the day before in *Le Monde*. It irritated me, despite the fact that it was doubtlessly a sign of respect because it indicated that his instinct for domination had found the opportunity for a skirmish that was more or less worth the effort. But although Michel and my father were the same age almost to the year, there was a generational gap between them. Michel was on the same level with young men like Hervé and me, and my father wasn't. My father was, however, when it came to literature, just as—if Gérard can be believed—Michel wasn't when it came to eating. When my father had read the manuscript of *The Bathroom* (*La Salle de bains*) and hit it off with Jean-Philippe Toussaint, who was two years younger than me, he used those two years as another way to lord over me, as grounds for competing with me even when it was a question of youth. And it's true that youth and life are linked in an obvious way to everything I retain about Michel and him. I was moved to noticed to what point my father remained a son because I understood the way he manipulated my relationship with my grandfather; and I was just as moved in grasping to what point he was a father, a prisoner of his paternal and uncertain love, unconfident as he was about what I was going to become. His omnipotence was a sham, and no one ever believed in it except me. I loved Michel, but not like a son. He helped me create the framework of a completely original relationship, which so many other future affections that developed as a result needed. He liberated me from what I hadn't chosen, from the integrated part of me but not the integral part. It felt as if he had a devotion to me that was discreet without being secret, loving but not anguished, which is the best you can receive. I liked the fact that my father was my father, as well as the fact that Michel wasn't.

A few days before Michel's death, *Libération* devoted all its initial pages to the publication of his last two books. The main lesson that the newspaper drew from them was that it was necessary to make your life a work of art. My father wasn't an artist or writer, but he put writers above everything else. He considered himself their representative, and instead of making his life a work of art, had made one of his profession. That is what Les éditions de Minuit was for him. Michel didn't claim to be a writer in the artistic sense, but he wouldn't have been the intellectual he was if his connection to art hadn't been as strong. For me, my father personified an association between art and commerce that is rarely so successful. Sometimes he was called greedy, and I'm certain he wasn't. If he made use of money, he used it as a strategy of domination and not out of any fetish for it. One day when he was emphasizing the disadvantages of his position of responsibility, I'd answered that he was compensated for it by the power he possessed. "Power, yes," he responded with a smile he couldn't restrain. It was an expression of delight, Scrooge McDuck's swimming in his pool filled with gold coins, or the way I imagined Saint-Simon's smile when after years and thousands of pages of bitterness he rapturously witnesses the humiliating degradation of Louis XIV's bastards, because I'd been reduced to thinking that my father was greedy for power, fetishism included. And it was logical. I could regret it but not find fault in it. The expression "jealous of his power" has everything in it of the pleonasm.

For Michel, strength was first and the rest followed from it. His way of listening to me, on the lookout for the slightest hold he could spot in order to help me, made that strength the sweetest and most necessary thing in the world. It was as if he had drawn from his work, so resonant with the theme of power, an unbelievable capacity for exercising it in personal relationships for the good of all—increasing the other's power and his own, or in any case, the other's. Things would jam up when my father wanted to do the same thing, obviously because of ties of filiation. There was never enough counterbalance to that pure power. I could say the very opposite: my father as well loved nothing so much as not dominating, being carried away by affection and admiration; but his standards were so high, as in the case of Beckett. To consider his own existence a happy one, he had to meet and find a way to facilitate the career and life of such a unique person. Being left alone was another of his preoccupations, but that resulted in a propensity for being bothered since by nature his profession distanced him from the ivory tower. One of his gestures, one of his expressions or phrases, could set my nerves on edge. Being his son came inches from making me dead set against him. Something you can't bear when it comes to a father is what he passes on to you. On the other hand, in my life I've never been irritated with Michel and doubtlessly not he with me, either, not counting the mischief Hervé and I indulged in when we acted like imbeciles in front of him, a motive that was unlikely to provoke reciprocity.

The way in which Michel brought up literature would always speak to me, whereas my father seemed particularly expert at appreciating and publishing it. Because of the way I'd been brought up, there was something sacred about books, but Michel had a way of making them prosaic and alive for me. According to my father, another person might have arrived at the same conclusions as me under the influence of Michel, but such an approach was impossible for my father and me.

That colleague who had tried to get the upper hand over me the day of my father's funeral, teaching me a lesson barely after he'd finished consoling me by expressing surprise I'd come to work, did it out of an ill-defined jealousy I've never been very good at countering. Maybe my books also incite that opposition; but my pedigree, which does have its advantages, was suddenly taking a rather undesirable turn. One day I played a small role as a philosophy teacher in a friend's film. It was kind of an affectionate private joke that required I be present for shooting in the places where he'd been raised and in the final cut of the film. The make-up girl asked me if I was related to the actor Lindon, who's my first cousin, and did her task with blatant hostility, as if I'd stolen that walk-on by nepotism from another more deserving. She didn't start behaving more appropriately until she'd understood that film wasn't my career. I was proud of being Michel's friend, as was the case with all my friends, since such a relationship went both ways and to an even greater extent in Michel's case. At the mere mention of his name, there were many who could understand the extent of my privilege. But I would have still remained my father's son even if I'd been ashamed of him or detested by him, and I was a tad unnerved to be proud of this despite the fact that my pride made sense simply because I loved and admired him.

"My condolences. But then, what are you doing here?" Being attacked by that cunning, roundabout remark irked me. In such circumstances a sensible armistice wouldn't have been out of place if I was detested; not to mention the fact that I'd been taken in by answering him, as if an older person (although not old enough to be my father) were educating me. A sly smile would have been a better reaction than the best rejoinder. I better understood Michel's joy when Hervé repeated a remark to him that elevated him all by himself to the rank of perversion. As an angle of attack, I would have preferred my former officemate's banal and unpleasant words, which I understand more or less today and can extrapolate from his ill-defined hostility: "You're a fag and a drug addict, and you're Jérôme Lindon's son."

5

Adalbert Stifter is an Austrian writer who was born in 1805 and died in 1868. I don't understand a word of German, and I'd never heard anything about him before I discovered a translation of one of his books on a desk when I first started working at *Le Nouvel Observateur*. I took it home and began to read it. The title of this story or novella is *Bachelors* (*Der Hagestolz*), and I was immediately fascinated by it. In it I discovered something that reminded me of *The Night of the Hunter*, the film directed by Charles Laughton. Stifter's text and Laughton's film interfaced in a kind of exaggerated classicism that was at once childish and mature. In my eyes this endowed them with uncompromising originality, as if their creations hadn't arisen from the same art as any other film or novel. I started reading the book to pass the time while I waited for a lover who was supposed to stop by my place, and it turned out I had gotten halfway through it by the time she became late, something I usually have little patience for. In this particular case, however, I was praying for her to be even later, detesting the idea of being interrupted as I read. As it happened, the girl arrived when I'd come to the end of the text; and she was also the one that night who informed me about the way another of her boyfriends had characterized me by an unexpected trio of vices that involved Michel.

My enthusiasm for *Bachelors* made it the most bought book in my life, because I offered copies to all my friends, including Gérard, Hervé and even Michel, to whom I rarely recommended readings. I also sang its praises to my father, although it didn't possess a high degree of the kind of originality of form he liked, and the writer was as unknown to him as he had been to me a week earlier. On the other hand, my mother had already read some of the earlier translations. All this wasn't enough for him to read the book immediately, but he'd been sufficiently impressed by my flight of enthusiasm to return to it a few days later. He'd talked about it with Sam who, naturally, was very familiar with Stifter, which isn't especially surprising because Stifter is one of the most revered writers in the German language (my interest in him would lead to discovering how highly Nietzsche, Herman Hesse and Peter Handke regarded him). Sam, who read German, had added that Stifter's most beautiful work was a long novel entitled *Indian Summer* (*Der Nachsommer*). I read all that I could of Stifter, always in a state of rapture. Little had been translated into French previously, but despite its title, *Bachelors* had its descendants, and to my greatest joy stories and collections of stories started to be published. Missing, however, was *Indian Summer*, and I kept hoping to read that title in publishers' listings of forthcoming translations. All the texts that were being translated were short, and I looked forward to the prospect of reading a long text, despite the fact that there were no signs of its happening. The charm of Stifter's works enchanted me even more when I discovered that he had wanted to be a painter for a long time before he'd started writing.

More than twenty years passed between the moment when I'd learned of the existence of Stifter and his famous novel and the publication of *Indian Summer*, which actually had been translated into French with the title *L'Arrière-saison*. The book was 650 pages long, and I was glad I could take it to Rome where

I was spending a few days of vacation with Rachid, who is fifteen years younger than me and was enjoying a residency at the villa Medicis as I had approximately ten years before with Hervé, who had tried in vain to snag an extra year by presenting himself as a graphic artist after a residence as a writer—like Stifter, but in reverse. Those twenty years of waiting must have prepared me to savor every shred of the book's charms, and despite the fact that even his most illustrious acolytes mentioned the boredom of certain passages, I was thrilled at every moment. Something was becoming strained, changing, in my relationship with Rachid around this time. We were inches away from arguing during this stay when I spoke to him at lunch about *Indian Summer* (he was familiar with Stifter, having also been entitled to his copy of *Bachelors*). And as if the way I talked was faithful to my reading, it brought tears to my eyes and almost to his. According to the description on its back cover, the novel "pursues an aesthetic and moral ideal with extreme ambition." The hero, who is the narrator, is a young man described in accord with the rules of a coming-of-age novel, but in addition to a young girl, he meets an old woman and an old man with mysterious links, and each near death. And yet, with Stifter, as it was in *Bachelors*, age creates youth, and without the aged, deprived of this circle and this context, the young man is completely lost, hampered by his own age, sensations and ambitions. In Rachid's eyes I was definitely not old, but I was certainly no longer that person who had fallen into the Stifterian magic potion when still young. And although I would have liked once more to recommend this reading to my father, who was now seventy-five years old, it was too late. He was already lying in what would become his deathbed, something I was beginning to suspect despite myself. It wasn't only the twenty years I'd had to wait for the translation that justified my emotion. In addition to the text itself, there was all that those twenty years had left behind.

After the appearance of my article, I happened to meet the publicist for the translation of *Indian Summer*, who thanked me kindly for it and added that the author of another article on the novel had told her he'd been ashamed of his after having read mine. I was touched by such a discreet publicist's sensitivity in repeating this to me. Moreover, the thought expressed by the author of the other article transported me back to the world of Stifter where such elegance is the norm. It also brought me back to my own world in which Stifter, despite my readings and articles, is when all is said and done merely a peripheral element. As Michel and I often spoke about literature, he had told me while I was explaining my taste for Faulkner, Conrad and Melville, how much Anglo-Saxon literature generally attracts a different kind of fan than German literature does. Michel was the counter-example of this. As a hyper-informed Germanist, he nonetheless thought so highly of *Under the Volcano* that it had been an immense compliment to Hervé when he compared him to Malcolm Lowry in his preface to the catalogue on Duane Michals. It was something I was convinced of despite the fact that I'd forgotten to take the text with me one day on rue de Vaugirard. When Michel and I had these conversations, I was barely familiar with Hermann Hesse, Thomas Mann, Hermann Broch and Stifter himself, not to mention Thomas Bernhard. Afterwards I regretted a thousand times—since regret has a thousand ways of manifesting itself—my not being able to match his readings of these authors with my own, letting him know I'd as well now tread Germanic paths. The nobility of the reaction of the author of the other article on *Indian Summer* made me think of Michel, not only because nobility reminded me of him but also because it confirmed my new competences in loving German, or Austrian, literature. My father, on the other hand, was no longer in any state to read anything, including the novel or my article.

One day Michel had sung the praises of my articles for reason of their irony. It had surprised me because, given the precise case from which he drew such a generalization, I hadn't realized anything of the sort to the extent that I'd even wondered how to take it, but not for a long time because I was certain I could always take well what he told me. When I'd published my first novel under a pseudonym and sent it to Jean Dubuffet, whom I adored and whom personally Michel didn't like, and when Dubuffet had responded with a splendid letter, I'd told Michel about answering Dubuffet's letter to tell him who I was, seeing that I'd already been thrilled to meet the painter, whom I also admire as a writer. And Michel had laughed, doubtlessly because he found the case of chatty anonymity to be grotesque; but this was a hearty, unpremeditated laugh, and I as well had simply found ridiculous the corner into which I'd painted myself. I had found it ironic because for me irony has always covered the entire field of my existence. When I left the family apartment to live alone, my mother had given me all my old report cards so that I could get rid of them for her, and I'd read the oldest that contained my teacher's judgment of my diction, about which she'd merely written, "Language very precise, sometimes ironic." I was six, and I would have liked to recall what kind of irony a child of six could have.

Evidently it had to do with my journalistic writing. Like the good boy in *Bachelors*, I had a tendency to look at what I was told like a story, initially impervious to any possible strategy behind it. My father would put down journalists even more than publishers, and I therefore had begun life with a great distrust for them. At the same time, he'd been involved in getting me an internship at *Le Nouvel Observateur* and then assured me that a profession was what you make of it and had also expressed his contentment when the magazine had ended up hiring me years later. This last event had delighted Michel when I told him about it. There were a host of interns and freelancers like me at *Le Nouvel Observateur*, and since the number of available pages was limited and co-opted by intellectuals who sometimes included Michel himself, the former would spend their time complaining about their articles not appearing. I had been happy to write a minimum of articles and was always in a cheerful mood without worrying about my status when it came to my unpublished texts, which eventually worked to make me the one who'd been hired first. And that strategy had so amused Michel that retrospectively I'd become proud about having concocted it. The fact that I'd been able to think in that way made him gloat about it as a description of the economic system. But the simple truth was that because of my pretensions and the prejudices I'd inherited from my father, the profession of journalism at that time stood so poorly in comparison to that of writer that my self-esteem, despite what I saw of it in others, was necessarily excluded from that profession. My irony was ontological and naïve. All I wanted was a place in a world where, I was discovering with humorless irony, I was still a stranger.

Long before meeting Michel, I'd adored not only the book *Madness and Civilization* (*Histoire de la folie*) itself but also the three-page preface he'd written for its rerelease in which he'd explained why it was impossible for him to draft a preface to such a text and concluded with lines that were suddenly in the form of a dialogue: "But you just created a preface." "At least it's short." This was a healthy relationship to theory, my idea of irony. The one whom it called into question was most often the ironist himself. In reading texts by Nietzsche, sometimes I couldn't understand whether what was being written was expressing its own thought or ridiculing those who thought that way. After Michel's death, I became more familiar with German literature and sometimes had the same uncertainty about Thomas Mann. I so loved *Joseph and His Brothers* (*Joseph und seine Brüder*) while being persuaded on a thousand different occasions of having read it the wrong way. But for me, Stifter, like Willa Cather in American literature, was beyond irony. I had no trouble imagining the detractors of these authors but thought their belief that they were making fun of these works only served to reveal their own meanness, just as those reading *Les Misérables* who would have snickered at Bishop Myriel and be certain he'd been conned by Jean Valjean, the idiot, were the type who would have stuck to this interpretation throughout the entire novel.

Indian Summer called to mind Michel without my knowing why. It wasn't just its assuaged and serene ferment or the aristocratic wisdom it evoked, and the theme of old age had nothing to remind me of Michel. It was something that had to do with me. It was like a coming-of-age novel written just for me, and it was the highest form of it there was. Stifter describes the two oldest characters as living "in happiness and constancy a kind of end of autumn that hadn't had any summer." My horrible adolescence had retarded my youth, and Michel's death had laid it to rest. At least that was what I imagined. I'd met Michel around the age when my father had met Samuel Beckett, even if I'd had to know him more than thirty years less than my father had known Sam. I identified with my youth and even youth in general. In my eyes Michel personified both, as my father was able to do in his own way. Meeting someone is always an event in life, and for me, this was so difficult for such a long time that such luck felt almost like a mythical adventure. Those brought up in the context of familial norms will always miss the chance of getting to know their parents or of their parents getting to know them. There was no natural, objective love at first sight nor any unencumbered apprenticeship with the other person. Love preexists on one side, and is necessitated on the other—it's a plus and it's a minus. Only adolescence had escaped me. Through happiness and constancy I suddenly understood how to live in a kind of late fall that wouldn't have had any spring, as if blessedly halted in summer.

When I'd met Rachid, I'd been sorry Michel and he didn't know each other. I imagined Michel would have adored him for a reason resembling his comparison of Hervé to Malcolm Lowry, for his quiet and raw unconventionality, his innocent autonomy. And so, during a moment of tension with Rachid that determined our future, I actually wasn't worried. I knew what to do. It was enough to count on him and on myself, on his love and mine, and things took care of themselves with a potential scorn for all convention. All I had to do was speak to him about *Indian Summer*, something I did because I couldn't help doing it; all I had to do was have confidence in Michel. In front of him I'd always felt like a child—not his, however—like a young man, and that feeling may very well last when I pass the age he had when he died, something that is arriving soon. I've appropriated the joy he expressed every time he opened the door for me on rue de Vaugirard. I felt capable of offering it in turn without even needing to pay attention to it. I'd taken a thousand things from him that became natural for me and for which I was grateful. That's the statutory difference between friend and father, an irony the latter is forced to taste bitterly. I felt gratitude for having become the former while I was still embittered about the latter. For me, changing seemed like advancing. My father was a fact; Michel had been an opportunity. Rachid shared in this legacy.

I was sure that Michel would have been happy about it, that it was exactly what he wanted in teaching me by practice those human relations through which I'd encountered Rachid, who was another expert in this matter, and generosity, unfortunately, had irony—which is what made it generosity—and my father must have had to feel this a thousand times when faced with me. Over the years, after it had come dangerously close to not being the case, Michel's death had left me more alive than ever, capable of seeing my father's end as grievous but not too much of a conscious schism. However, what I knew of the circumstances of Stifter's death came back to me. On January 26, 1868, at sixty-two, after a thousand torments, suffering abominably (cancer or cirrhosis of the liver), the author of so many masterpieces of apparently infinite serenity had slit his throat with a razor and had died only two days later. "Ah, Bartleby! Ah, humanity!" Herman Melville had written at the end of his most astounding story to which I'd devoted my masters at my university. Ah, irony! Ah, serenity!

6

Gérard gave me a cap the other day, and I was annoyed—I who never am. "He knows very well I don't wear one," I said as justification to Rachid, who was laughing at my irritation about receiving a gift from my most peace-loving friend as if it were a declaration of war. Without even having tried it on, I put it away in a closet where it has stayed. Clothing isn't my thing, and I aspire to nothing more than all-purpose simplicity. I remembered, however, that I was wearing one—a cap—the first time I saw Michel.

Properly speaking, I met Michel before the rue de Vaugirard, even if it wasn't a real encounter. My father had entrusted a review to me, and I decided to share direction with a Swiss friend, Denis, whom I knew from some texts he'd published. We'd asked for an interview with Michel Foucault, who'd told us to come to his place at the end of an afternoon. Denis and I had agreed to meet in front of the building in order to arrive together. I was early, as usual, and Denis kept me waiting inordinately long. At the agreed time for the meeting, he still wasn't there, so I began walking up to the apartment by myself, since I thought it was too impolite to be late when you were asking for a kind of favor from such a personality. Denis had been lost and only rang a full twenty minutes later, while I was already inside the apartment. That time, Michel hadn't produced any particular effect on me. I was too intimidated to be in the presence of Michel Foucault and annoyed and worried about Denis's absence. There was no interview; Michel politely sent us packing. Talking about that episode a single time required years of intimacy. Michel told me that he'd been prejudiced against me. Since I'd replaced Tony Duvert as head of the review, Michel had figured that I'd had my father boot out Duvert so I could substitute my little friend for him, and Michel hadn't any desire to support such nepotism.

But there had also been one more encounter beforehand that hadn't really been one, and we never discussed that one. After acing my *bac*,[1] I was still living at my parents, had an enormous amount of time as a student and didn't know anyone. Getting my *bac* hadn't miraculously blown the whistle ending my hellish adolescence even if university was going to help in that regard. At that point I was more confident in my literary than in my sexual tastes. I knew that Michel Foucault was teaching a course open to all at the Collège de France. I even knew that the rules of the institution specified he only teach a seminar with a dramatically reduced student body in which I would therefore have more of a chance of getting noticed. At the beginning of the semester, I went to the first class of that session of the seminar. There weren't many of us, and Michel was attempting to discourage us. Even so, you had to fill out a form, which I did, glad it required us to include our names since I was proud of mine. I'd absorbed our family's elitism in a manner that was a bit skewed. I wasn't at all under the impression that my father was famous—like an actor or soccer player. What child is fascinated by an editor whose publishing house doesn't even carry his name? No classmate had ever asked if I was from his family. But I did consider the fact that he might be famous and respected in a select, more refined milieu, to which Michel Foucault belonged.

---

1. Translator's note: *bac* = *baccalauréat*, an exam taken at the end of the French equivalent of high school, passing of which allows the candidate to pursue a higher education.

At our house we weren't accustomed to making fun of my father. However, there was an accepted joke that consisted in attributing to him phrases that the character Agamemnon sings (after being introduced by the words "the bearded king arriving drunk, arriving drunk...") in the famous "Marche des Rois" of *La Belle Hélène*: "I've said enough I think in saying my name" or "And this name alone is enough, is enough, enough to say much more." With a simplicity that was sometimes affected, since Offenbach is rarely the favorite musician of music lovers, my grandfather adored Offenbach, who was part of our family culture. Another a barb consisted in placing the names of Offenbach's popular librettists Meilhac and Halévy in the same list as Beckett, Duras, Robbe-Grillet, Deleuze, Bourdieu, Robert Pinget and Claude Simon, who all came to our house by way of my father. This kind of thing placed thorns in my wretchedness, my being something of a snob, and not even aware of it. When Michel perused the form I'd filled out, he showed no more sign of interest in me than he had had in seeing me. That was enough to distance me. Even if I can sometimes be tenacious, I was reminded of myself many years later in reading a conversation with Jean Yanne that declared, "I'm the opposite of Bernard Tapie. At the first obstacle, I give up."

My father was always concerned with elegance. My mother often bought him his clothing, as she now does for me. Shortly before that period, he'd gotten hold of a cap and never left home without it, as if it had become indispensable. Since I've always thought of hats as absurd accessories, this impressed me all the more. The only real taste I had for clothes was for drab sweaters that were too large, roomy and comfortable enough to bunch in folds. The affair of my father's cap would teach me there was another more social use for clothing, and I wore one for a few weeks. It was atop my head when I went to the seminar at the Collège de France, where it's fanciful power of seduction didn't work.

I did the right thing in not waiting for Denis on the day of the second of my first real spurious encounters with Michel. He told me much later about being part of a jury one year with my grandfather. A taxi was supposed to take the two of them to the place, as well as a third man. When their car arrived at the place the third man lived, he wasn't waiting downstairs, keeping the driver, Michel and my grandfather waiting for several minutes. If what Michel said is true, as the seconds passed in the face of that rudeness, fury poured from every pore of my grandfather, to such an extent that Michel almost became worried about him, an incident he spiced up for me and made entertaining. It's true that one of my grandfather's brothers, a grand uncle whom I hardly knew, collapsed one evening in a restaurant and couldn't be revived. From what I was told, he died of rage, exasperated by the faulty service.

Just one time, Michel, Daniel, Hervé, his boyfriend Thierry and I went to the theater together. The play was being performed in the suburbs, and Michel drove us there. Barely an hour after the beginning of the show, there was a bomb threat, and we had to evacuate the theater. Outside, all of us were enthusiastic: the play, the staging—everything—was wonderful. Perhaps the interruption had spoiled it all, but after another half hour of the show, during intermission, Michel and I found the play so uninteresting that its staging no longer mattered; the only thing to do was to leave. Daniel and Thierry weren't against it, but Hervé was still under his first impression. Since a decision to leave early called for unanimity, we all stayed. The play had only restarted for less than five minutes when Hervé, who sat next to me, was now in agreement with the rest of us, but it had become impossible to move. Actors in warrior costumes, armed to the teeth and shouting, were surging through the audience from every corner of the room, and fleeing would have created a comic effect that seemed like an act of sabotage, as we murmured, "Excuse, me, sorry, sorry." Staying until the end felt like torture. Our minds were completely disengaged, without the slightest interest in what might happen onstage or in the theater, and our boredom nearly reached a level of hysteria. The ride back was grim. Michel was exasperated as if a delay had robbed him of time. No matter how much Daniel tried time and again to relax the atmosphere, no one dared open his mouth. Michel remained mum in order not to say anything unpleasant— I'd never seen him in such a state and never would again. He let us off on the Champs-Élysées so that all three of us could go to dinner without them, and he went home with Daniel.

Shortly before *To the Friend Who Did Not Save My Life* appeared, I was in Sao Paulo at Bernardo's. A week before my departure, Hervé had suggested I reread the book in proofs in case I had any suggestions, and as a result the text was fresh in my mind. At my first reading, I'd been so happy to see something about Michel brought back to life that I hadn't stopped to consider the effect that the novel and the passages about Daniel would have on him. I hadn't remarked on that immediately either at the second reading, but short as the deadline now was I did have some suggestions. However, at the time, getting hold of a telephone in Brazil was an adventure and Bernardo didn't have one. Calling from the post office was too ambitious for me, given my timidity and my weak mastery of Portuguese. It was only when I got back that I told Hervé that as far as I was concerned he could take out certain phrases that would be a concession to Daniel without it diminishing the novel. He would have done it, he answered, if I'd suggested it earlier; but the book was in production and now it was impossible to change anything at all. The most important sentence that I wanted him to censor concerned the fact that Michel was often beside himself when Daniel was late. I thought it was useless to inflict that on the survivor, although there was nothing surprising about such exasperation between two people who were so close. Moreover, I had the feeling that Michel could have been a member of my family, when it came to the issue of tolerance for lateness.

When he himself risked being late for a meeting at his place, he'd merely tell me to wait inside, since between stays I kept the key, which was still in my pocket the day he died. Twenty-five years later, I responded too snappishly to a friend who used our friendship to justify never being on time for our meetings by maintaining that there were people for whom being late was the only way of taking their time. Michel unfortunately found another, definitive way. Everyday, I wait for the moments when he materializes inside me to comfort me with his only existence, which is in the past.

Five years before meeting Michel, I knew Roland Barthes, who was probably one of the only other great names whom my father regretted not publishing. Tony Duvert, a Minuit author, had received the prix Médicis in the jury that Barthes had just become part of, and it was thanks to his support that the result had been possible. My father had invited Barthes to dinner at the house when I was eighteen, and I had been there. I certainly wasn't wearing my cap inside, but I hit it off with Barthes even so, who invited me to his seminar, as a result of which I saw him every week. I was younger than the other participants and didn't arrive until the year was underway. I was intimidated and rarely spoke a word. At the beginning of summer, I'd sent a few lines to excuse myself for not being able to attend the dinner at the end of the course. Barthes' answer was that it wasn't important to be there and that there would be other occasions. "This seminar is waiting for you," he'd written, "as am I" (right away he'd used the informal "you" to address me). I was late, and that lateness was permanent. He was expecting a certain act from me, more than words, and when I balked, I was expelled without delay from that world. No other seminar session ever welcomed me, which I found both justifiable and rude. It was as if I'd suddenly become a nonentity.

At the opening of an exhibition devoted to him decades after his death, I congratulated the curator and drew her attention to a young man in a raincoat in an enormous group photo of the seminar. "Yes, he's the only one we couldn't identify," she told me. It was I, of course.

I only saw Barthes one time after we hadn't gone to bed together. He was one of the guests at the evening of the nude but not naked Japanese dancer. Thierry and I had arrived earlier at rue de Vaugirard, in order to help if that came up. Michel sent us to get some bottles from the cellar, which required you to leave the building before reentering it. During our short walk outside, we fell upon Barthes as he was arriving. In seeing me, his face registered surprise as pronounced as the way astonishment is indicated in a cartoon or comic strip. He couldn't get over it to such an extent that his reaction would have been rude if it hadn't been so spontaneous. It was instinctively insulting, doubtlessly because he was thinking I would have had to end up as one of homosexuality's rejects and only a miracle, which had therefore happened, could have pulled me out of nothingness. Although not by design or strategy, we exchanged not a word during the evening. I never spoke to Michel about this, and he must not have suspected that we knew each other. And now that I had developed this unexpected relationship with Michel, a kind of compassionate megalomania made me feel sorry not so much for myself, since I had Michel, but for Barthes. He as well would have been able to draw something from me. Curious as it seemed, I felt he'd lost more than me because Michel had saved me. I found it sad, to repeat an expression that a boy in the following millennium often employed. He was a boy more than twenty years younger than me, and I ended up no longer seeing any other way out of our relationship than trying to behave toward him as Barthes had acted in my regard (although he didn't leave my life as easily as I had Barthes').

Michel only spoke to me once about Barthes' death. Run over by a van while leaving the Collège de France, he'd never gotten out of the hospital where, according to rumor, he'd been more or less allowed to die. Michel, who had himself spent a few days in the hospital after having been run over while leaving his home, told me that people don't realize the effort it takes to survive in the hospital, and that allowing yourself to die is the de facto condition of hospitalization. You have to struggle to fight against it. In support of his theory, he added that people, on the contrary, had imagined Barthes enjoying a long, happy old age, like a Chinese sage. After Michel's death, I saw his aged master who'd been struck by my utter dismay. Since he was old—too old for his liking—he'd insisted how lucky Michel had been to die young in full possession of his faculties. He'd wanted to console me with such words, but it was clear that he found that his own supposedly happy old age had gone on awfully long.

My father was seventy-five when he died, and that helped me to think that all in all he had had a good life. My older brother wasn't at the funeral, and it became my duty to say Kaddish. Sometimes my father would do this at Jewish funerals even when he wasn't considered the appropriate person according to the rite, because he knew it by heart and in such cases the sons of the deceased didn't always. I no longer read Hebrew, which I'd learned just for my Bar Mitzvah. A friend who had just lost a parent had given me a phonetic transcription of the prayer. So I read sounds that were incomprehensible in French, although repetition lent them the sense and beauty of a solemn poem, as one of my uncles, more versed than I in Judaism, remarked to me when I'd finished. While agreeing, I realized I'd forgotten to put my yarmulke on my head. It had remained in my pocket, and I took it out to show my uncle what a stupid mistake I'd made. He was amused, because he must have believed I'd purposely done without it as a secular rebellion, yet preferred it to be interpreted as featherbrained stupidity and therefore had brought one with me. Incidentally, religiously speaking, all I'd needed to do was to avoid having a bare head. A simple cap would have fit the bill.

7

"But they'll never let you enter, my lambs," Michel told us one day when he had dressed to go to a bar more hardcore than those we frequented and Hervé and I were acting as if we wanted to come along. It was a joke because we weren't muddling categories and had no intention of going there. The term "lambs" possessed its usual affectionate connotation, but distance had been added to it: we lambs weren't part of this world. Our youth would serve no advantage if we weren't following the required dress code. The fact that it gave us no advantage over Michel had pleased us like justice itself.

I'd noticed a few years before that this wasn't exactly the case. During my trip to New York with Gérard and Marc where I'd lost my LSD virginity, we'd also gone one night to the Mine Shaft, a gay sadomasochistic bar of such repute at the time that we'd wanted to catch the show there, even my friends who weren't reckoning on meeting anyone there at all. To be honest, I wasn't looking to get off there either. Despite my curiosity, I was afraid of all the hardcore scenes I'd heard went down in such a place, as if there were a slight risk I'd be pulled into the action despite myself in a place where previous consent was the assumed rule. We had trouble finding the place. It was in the western part of Greenwich Village, in the meatpacking district by the docks and warehouses. It was three in the morning, and everything was deserted. There was nowhere more disreputable, but ignorance banished insecurity; we were more worried about finding our way and what could happen there once we found the place than about the risk of wandering around in the middle of the night. Eventually we fell upon it, and they let us in despite our jeans and T-shirts. Inside we'd noticed that we were a lot younger than all the other men, and we hadn't stayed long because the action in that kind of place is only exciting if you're more prepared to participate in it than we were. Also, nobody was interested in us, and our identity as intruders was glaringly evident. Even as voyeurs, we weren't convincing. When I'd told Michel about it, he'd been flabbergasted that they hadn't slammed the door in our faces as he would have clearly done in a similar case, since age can't outdo practical experience.

Although I kept him up to date on my adventures out of a conciliatory obligation that seemed to suit him, Michel was a lot more discreet. I only remember how he spoke about Daniel when telling me that after so many years sex certainly wasn't any longer the main element of their relationship and how that had made me regain my composure and opened new horizons. And how, one evening when I visited him on rue de Vaugirard, he was still feeling the effects of a session the day before when he'd brought back a young man. When the S&M ritual had barely begun, the boy gleefully showed how much he was into it by declaring, "This is too cute," after which, Michel laughingly told me, he himself hadn't been able to go on. Despite their reputation, in so much as partners of elaborate sexual games twinks aren't worth a damn.

The fact that I never had sex with either Michel or Hervé—they were my only two friends with whom it had cropped up but never happened—was actually an additional bond among us three. Since AIDS kills, the one with whom I hadn't at first wanted to have sex and the one who hadn't wanted to have sex with me prevented me from regretting those unconscious blunders. It's a disgrace, but that's the way it is.

By roundabout but indisputable pathways Michel's death had led me to meet Bernardo; and Hervé's death, Rachid. Nor could I get over being able to lose people who were so close to me and finding others as a result; it was moving for me to see my loves linked in such a way across the years. Later, I thought about the fact that my father's death had itself been a founding element in a disastrous relationship with a boy whom I called "my adored catastrophe" and who, despite the intensity and intimacy of our bond, always refused sex—with less affection than Michel and a cruder will for strength, he never stopped his way of telling me in reference to his own ass, "I'll never let you inside, my lamb." And while this torture was in force, Michel's absence was even more apparent because I couldn't call on him to help me get out of it, never again. Naturally, I didn't miss my father in that way. After Michel's funeral, I had seen Gilles Deleuze for some time, whose words at the funeral home had so touched me. Once, when I told him how my father aggravated me at moments, he'd reassured me that he was sure it was reciprocal. Starting then, I'd incorporated that potential reciprocity into all my relationships; but when it came to issues of sex and my father, our total silence was mutual. Even so, wouldn't reciprocity have been the strongest when it came to the subject of love? Wouldn't my father himself have begun calling me his adored catastrophe if such an immodest vocabulary had been part of his register?

In analyzing his wonderful posthumous letter over the span of years, I could decode in his request to forget him a kind of wish for a post-mortem peace of mind for us both, in the tone of teens who need to feel close enough to say, "Stop thinking about me all the time, please," "Let go." I'd waited too long to let go of

my adored catastrophe, and I would have been an adored catastrophe in my father's eyes not because of my own lacks but
through a kind of double bind characteristic of paternity, where
the child is either not doing what was wanted for him, leading to
disappointment, or does it, leading to submission. Did the
Williams sisters' father, who'd always wanted to turn them into
the tennis champions they became, not sometimes suppose that
they would have been even stronger if they'd told him and his
rackets at the age of five to go fuck off? Or did he think they'd
proved an even greater strength by achieving a dream that hadn't
been theirs from the very start? My father's hope that I'd give him
grandchildren, in any case, had been disillusioned quickly
enough. Even his talent for discussion would be powerless to
convince me. He'd understood it when he'd realized that I didn't
want to get married, when I didn't even know that I was telling
that to myself (but he'd seen it just as Michel had). "Fatherhood,
I'll never let you inside, my lamb." From then on, my sex life no
longer interested him, which spared him a thousand anxieties.
All he regretted was the possible damage my book might create
for family respectability in referring to the subject. It was my
literary sexuality that was the problem.

As a child, I still wasn't aware that because sexuality played such
an explicit part in Alain Robbe-Grillet's work he had become my
favorite and least intimidating guest of all the writers who came
to dinner. I experienced him as the only one who had a relationship of camaraderie with my father, in addition to
everything else. It was that much more justified because they
were about the same age and had worked together to make Les
éditions de Minuit what it had become, had shared something
important in their life as young men. Long after, it had pleased
me to hear Michel cite Robbe-Grillet first among those authors
who were at ease in their work, thereby establishing the most

positive rapport; and the figure of Alain himself gave those words personal meaning for me. He was also the only writer from Minuit whose family we knew, not only his wife but also his sister, and even his parents. In his trilogy *Les Romanesques*, which is in some sense autobiographical, Robbe-Grillet describes his deceased mother and talks about rehearing her voice. I was stunned when I reached those lines, because as I read them, I too reheard that voice that was as distinctive as Alain's, although I only remembered meeting the woman five to ten times. I'd never thought I'd read the autobiography of a writer in his sixties and remember his mother. It was like realizing to what point literature was for all eternity linked to my life, not only by texts but also by life itself.

I had always been familiar with some of Mme Robbe-Grillet's remarks. They had become legendary in our family. *Le Voyeur* had appeared the year of my birth. It's her son's second published novel, and a sex crime that may have happened is the central element of the plot. At the time, she said to my mother, "It's really a very beautiful book. The only thing I don't like about it is that Alain is the one who wrote it." In my own way, I was rapidly also becoming a writer who speaks about sex but was confronted by parents who conformed more to the norm when it came to this context and in their appreciation of my texts were in no great hurry to sort out what had to do with literature and what with me. At the time of the publication of my first novel, my conflict with my father was resolved when he decided to have my manuscript read anonymously by Robbe-Grillet, whose enthused reaction delighted me. My childhood affection for him would endure as well, precisely because he was the person whom it was simpler for me to talk about sex with, before I was surrounded by my own circle of friends. Once having read my book, with perfectly sincere nonchalance, he'd been the only one to dare question me about the autobiographical nature of the sordid practices I was depicting. And although he wasn't homosexual, he explained to me why he was so sure of his opinion in a way that afterwards allowed us to mention the subject as if it were the most ordinary in the world. After the affair of the manuscript, when I saw him in the presence of my father or my mother, he never stopped his talk about the beautiful boys whom he was aware I knew, his only reason for bringing them up. He wanted my opinion of some of them, whether I knew this one or that one very well. He was, in other words, cheerfully referring to the fact that we were or had been lovers. He behaved more or less the same way with my parents as Hervé and I had with Michel when he was leaving for his S&M bar. However, the rapport wasn't the same, and my parents responded to it less affectionately than Michel had, not at all, in fact. The word *lover* had never been too much part of their vocabulary, but it was certainly not in these circumstances that I'd have become their twink. Alain had fun making them feel uncomfortable as if it were a practical joke. Even in his eighties, he as well always personified something about youth for me.

Moreover, in my eyes sexuality linked Alain and my father. The innuendos about me had vaster implications when my mother was present. During the time when Les éditions de Minuit depended most of all on a fighting spirit, they'd gone on trips together that I suspected they sometimes turned into heterosexual joyrides. As quite a young man, I'd been uncomfortable lunching with my father and one of his friends from his teenage years when the latter spoke about their adventures together. I hadn't felt that way when I imagined such things shared with Alain. After my father died, Alain's wife Catherine published a memoir about that time, revealing that sexual connections with the Robbe-Grillets had gone beyond my previous imaginings. She had already put out a book about her sadomasochistic experiences while my father was alive, and to defend it she'd appeared on the TV show *Apostrophes* anonymously, wearing a veil but easy to identify. Such marketing publicity for sadomasochism was badly received by my parents, seeing that she was violating the rules of discretion more than undermining morality. I wasn't far from thinking the same. But when Catherine, over the age of seventy, mounted the stage for a show focusing on sadomasochism and from which a record was cut, I was staggered—for me that kind of lack of tact seemed admirable. Rightly or wrongly, I imagined that Michel would have been impressed, too. Maybe he would have laughed, but not necessarily mockingly. Who knows whether he would not have stuck out his lower lip in the same charming expression of appreciation he'd had in mentioning my grandfather's unexpected recommendation for acquittal?

In *Les Romanesques* Robbe-Grillet also writes that my father, when he knew him, would not stop telling a story that only he found funny and that left everybody else ill at ease. It's about a father with his child in his arms, throwing him higher and higher to the child's joy, always catching him at the last moment. Then he throws him especially high and at the last moment doesn't catch him in order to perfect the child's education by letting him know never to trust anyone. I'd never heard the story before reading it. Later, I equated my father's absolute lack of trust in others with how incredibly cautious he was, and I felt sorry about the kind of upbringing he must have had. Sometimes he managed his relationship with me by letters that resembled deeds executed by a notary, not exactly something to kick-start effusiveness. Despite this, my entire childhood I had the feeling I was his favorite. Whether by unconscious imitation or by reversal, it was from him that I drew my need for wholehearted trust between lovers and couldn't tolerate any relationship that was too uncertain or combative.

I was immediately convinced when Michel told me you could often find ill intentions in the aphorisms of moralists.

What instantly came to mind was La Rochefoucauld's too transparent remark about it being "more shameful to mistrust one's friends than to be misled by them." What pleased Michel about a relationship was its singularity, and its strategy consisted in sustaining originality. For me, knowing him simultaneously encouraged the praxis and non-praxis of sex. In opposition to La Rochefoucauld's famous aphorism claiming that some people would never have been in love if they hadn't ever heard about it, Michel managed to see to it that I could be in love without knowing I was, due to the fact that I'd never heard it said that love could be like that. I could still savor the benefits, missing nothing as a result of my ignorance. My father's obsessional will to power was actually limiting his freedom, be it only the freedom to let live—gently, democratically—his connection with me, according to the same reasoning he used in assuring me that a magazine with two hundred thousand subscribers could very well be more financially independent than another without any, but still was less so because it would have to employ marketing and publicity to keep from losing the financial value of such readers. (He stayed faithful to that line of reasoning by preventing his personal expansionism from rubbing rub off on the number of books Minuit published, always preferring instead to snag new battles for himself.) On the contrary, one of the most fascinating things about Michel was being the opposite of a colonizer. He could not have a paternal relationship with me because he was the antithesis of a father. He'd never nip—even in the bud—a so-called colonial subject's revolt.

When Michel was in the hospital and we did not yet know he would get out of it only to go to the funeral home, Daniel witnessed a discussion with his editor during which Michel forgot the title of one of his own books and did everything he could to try to hide it in order not to cause worry. Now, the text in question was *Ceci n'est pas une pipe* (*This Is Not a Pipe*), in reference to the painting by Magritte in which that sentence appears under the image of a pipe. It has always made me think of Robbe-Grillet because that problematic graphic has to do with the kind of narrative theorized by the Nouveau Roman. Daniel had fleetingly drawn the conclusion—and why not?—that this lapse of memory came from Michel's conviction of having caught HIV during oral sex in a San Francisco bathhouse.[1] He would make use of his invitations to the United States to frequent such establishments. They afforded an anonymity that made them pleasanter for him than those in France, where his fame meant he'd immediately be identified. His books had given him a reputation and influence whose effects he was trying to restrict, to extract from his daily life. In saying his name—and even in not saying it—he always said too much.

After reading the manuscript of my first novel that was going to create so much stir with my father, Michel talked to me about the sexual freedom he'd discovered over there. I answered by saying that sadly, when it came to that, my body wasn't on the same level. It was a small confession to which Michel merely responded by saying, "Of course," the way you would say, "That would be too easy," as if, in comparison, he obviously needed to cause himself more trouble than that to liberate his own body. Around the same period, when Alain Robbe-Grillet acted as mediator between my father and me, I spoke to Alain about my father's puritanism and the word surprised him, not being at all adequate in his point of view. Later, when things between my father and me had settled down, I had a rare intimate discussion with him in which I mentioned feeling puritanical on a thousand

---

1. The connection between *pipe*, meaning "pipe" in English, and Foucault's conviction can only be understood by knowing that *faire la pipe* ("do the pipe," or perhaps "piping") is French slang for "giving a blowjob."

occasions. "That's something that's very important for me to know," he answered mysteriously with satisfaction.

At the time I was editing the review *Minuit*, I would stop at the publishing house on a Sunday afternoon to read the texts that had come in. There wasn't another soul there. The office I was using on the fourth floor was a room of about a hundred square feet that Robbe-Grillet had occupied for a period when he was young. It was next to my father's. One day I walked into my father's office to pace up and down and eventually sat on the leather couch. It was located next to the place where my father sat when he was there, instead of opposite it, where some armchairs had been positioned; and I'd never wondered about how it was used. This was before I knew Michel, who I'd learn had been aware of the couch's attractions for a long time. However, something about the texture of the material tempted me. It felt so nice against my hands. To get a better feel of that animal skin, I lowered my pants so that my thighs could take advantage of it. The sensation persisted. So I took off every article of clothing for an even better sample, afraid that someone—my father, obviously— would suddenly appear, but reassured by the floor I was on, which would provide time to react. There was no interruption before I reached a climax, the origins of which escaped me, given the fact that the ending only produced a second of satisfaction. I put my clothes back on, feeling ashamed, piddling, the opposite of totally fulfilled. Never again would I do anything like that, although I would have had a lot of trouble defining it. From then on, besides one-on-one encounters, I became familiar with the backrooms, dark cellars whose architecture was less appealing than their population and where homosexuality was being practiced in broad daylight—or rather—broad night. It was a kind of homosexuality that Michel was foremost in helping me construct, eventually making it both my pleasure and my sanctuary, a way of opening up and withdrawing, my land and my lair.

8

One day when I was a teenager, my father laid into Michel Foucault in front of me. He reproached him for having quoted from *The Unnamable* (*L'Innommable*) in his welcoming speech at the Collège de France without mentioning Beckett's name. In the written text, those sentences are enclosed in quotation marks, so there's not the slightest doubt that Michel wasn't trying to plagiarize. But I didn't know him at the time and didn't feel the slightest need to defend him. I should add that totally agreeing with my father seemed the minimum I owed not only to filial affection but also to his image for me—it was for my welfare, too. I understood that my father's criticism of Foucault came from the fact that he wasn't published at his house but couldn't be thought of as an unimportant figure. What I sometimes call my father's wish for omnipotence can be just as well thought of as a quest for perfection. Concocting an answer I thought would please him the most—not by flattering him but by consoling and comforting him to stop this shortcoming from being one—I finally said, "I wonder if Sam even knows the name Michel Foucault." I thought I'd done well, but my father's face took on its familiar exasperated expression. I'd gone too far, as my mother sometimes did with the same goal in mind, leading to the same result. As better proof of her support, she would take a swipe at a current adversary by spouting criticism so improbable that it was worse than saying nothing, the same way that a senseless compliment can humiliate.

My father told me one time that our mother spoke about novels as if they were real life and about life as if it were a novel. To me the reproach seemed applicable to a thousand occasions, a thousand emotions. I wasn't implying by my remark that Sam was an illiterate but that he was on a level that made him inaccessible to celebrities of an inferior order. At the house, despite how close we became with him, he was a sort of god verging on the conceptual, and in the order of things gods need not be informed about the vagaries of editorial and intellectual life. My father, on the other hand, had day-to-day and affectionate contact with Sam. When he'd announced his death to me he'd had tears in his eyes describing how Sam had kissed his hand at the end, in spite of the fact that my father clearly believed he should have been the one gratefully kissing Sam's hand. He'd not at all been a divinity for my father but unequivocally a human being— albeit an exceptional one. Sam read newspapers and contemporary authors; obviously he knew who Foucault was. It was too stupid.

In addition, for me writers belonged to a blessed race. Philosophers let fly with all their intelligence, but only the good writers attained another world. Maybe that presumption was ridiculous, but my ambition to become part of that world prevented me from doubting the value of that community. Michel told me later that when a great twentieth-century writer expressed the same adolescent theory against him and to his face, all he'd answered was, "Yes." He was implying that the others who were deprived of such a gift might have been miserable but had the right to live and work nonetheless. To me, the authors I knew at the time were like my parents: I'd never really met them since they'd always been there. I was more familiar with their works than most teenagers, and later, young men, of my age. However, as people their principal identity was as guests at dinners at home. In that familial but formal context they came from a world of magic reinforced by the fact that their ties to my father existed out of the apartment and were part of his work—in other words, yet another world. As writers, all these exceptional beings cut their meat, allowed themselves to be served wine or had a second helping of dessert, like extraterrestrials who were only tied to Earth at certain instances because of their links to my father. I had to be aware of how lucky I was to know them and take care not to take advantage of it at the same time. I had to keep from being noticed, hide my significance, being officially included in this circumstance because of the importance of my father. Michel Foucault was someone who had never come to dinner, and Minuit hadn't published any of his books. My remark was just a way of making him pay the price for it.

A few weeks after my father died, the Syndicat national de l'édition organized a tribute where Jacques Chirac took the floor in his role as president of the Republic. I was introduced to the President as the son just as the Republican Guard marched in front of him, stood at attention and handed him an envelope that he took without a word. I was shocked for a moment, because it seemed like a rude gesture. I often felt the same when I visited my father at the publisher's and noticed how miserly he was with "please" and "thank you" to his secretary or any of the other employees. He seemed even more so when I started working at *Libération*, where even the rank and file could insult superiors. To me, the tone my father used with his workers seemed to come from another time. Eighteen months before his death, Les éditions de Minuit won more of an abundance of literary prizes than ever before, and several employees of the house took the trouble of telling him how happy they were for him. Because he told me about it, he must have actually been touched. Being on the same level with Literature didn't prevent him from being a boss and trying to be the best one possible. What struck me was actually something obvious.

As flattered as my father might have been, I still thought he would have been shocked that the president of the Republic did for him what it never did for any of his authors. The market or the vagaries of literary history could pay tribute to a publisher and so could any writer, but not the government. More than ten years before, I'd read the correspondence between Proust and Gaston Gallimard in which the writer chastises his publisher because his house had turned down *Swann's Way* (*Du côté de chez Swann*) even though it was enthusiastic about the rest of *Remembrance of Things Past*. I'd enjoyed the book so much that I lent it to my father because it had a myriad of reasons to interest him. He brought it back, had liked it and said, "It made me admire Gaston Gallimard even more. Because I'd have told that Proust to go to hell." The idea wasn't that far away from Beckett chucking manuscripts into the garbage chute for him, a mind-blowing thought but one that I found fantastic; as if the triumph of literature was all very well, but not to the point of needing to bore yourself stiff. Since the first unlettered person who happened to come along would have known you couldn't just consider Proust a loathsome piece of crap, my father had displayed the opposite affectation of fighting in favor of the purity of writing. Being right or wrong was becoming the least of his concerns. Such a thing didn't call for the president of the Republic showing up. It's true that my father was only talking, because he never could have read a manuscript by Proust before it was published, but talk matters when you're speaking to a son.

One day when I had to maneuver Minuit's pawns in Michel's presence, he told me that he wasn't a snob when it came to publishers. No kidding, since any of them would have moved heaven and earth to publish him and those where his books appeared weren't exactly the shoddiest. I was learning about another type of author-publisher relationship from him, and as the years passed he was willing to tell me about the vicissitudes of his publications. Generally, there were hardly any conclusions I should be drawing from the supposedly theoretical opinions about publishers brought up when I was around, because they could all be explained away as resentment or envy. Such feelings had no place when Michel was talking to me about the subject. There was the story about the republication of a former book that he felt very strongly about. He thought he'd been conned when a publisher took abusive advantage of a contract, and there was nothing Michel could do about it because the publisher knew he'd lost his copy of the contract. His only recourse was to tell the publisher what he thought of him: "You're a gob of spit." Naturally I didn't recognize my father in that assessment, because for me he was beyond reach of any justified insult.

After the success of Marguerite Duras' *The Lover* (*L'Amant*), she and my father had a falling out. A female colleague at the paper interviewed her for the next release of one of her books and afterwards told me, tactfully, to prevent my being humiliated, how Duras had vented against my father. "She told me that he was a thief," my confederate told me. "Right then she glanced at my hands. 'Such a beautiful ring must be very valuable,' she said. 'You're going to see Jérôme Lindon? Watch out.'" The notion that my father, like a pickpocket, was going to pilfer the ring of a woman he'd neither seen nor knew and palm it off on a fence, unless he had his own network for moving loot, didn't offend me at all because it was funny. On the other hand, I was sorry those sentences weren't going to appear in the article since I thought they could only work in his favor. As wily as he could be when it came to such a notion, for me he was honesty itself—a rascal, yes, but only in the playful sense of the word. That was the maximum reproach I was ready to concede. When I was younger, wise as he was from experience, he told me that good conduct is always necessary because it's the most convenient, and I had complete confidence in his know-how because convenience later became a cardinal virtue for me, too.

The hate and jealousy toward Michel were more rational, provoked by his central interests and the positions he took. They were, nevertheless, incomprehensible to me. I thought that instead the entire planet should have shown its gratitude when faced with a person of such value. In my opinion, like Victor Hugo he could have written, "It surprises me to be the object of hate, / After suffering and working so much." I don't actually believe Michel was surprised, but I was; I was indignant, actually. The fact that he was a universally recognized writer and his dedication to his work combined to make him a kind of symbol that had to be defended independently of my love for him, a Sam of another generation with whom I had a different kind of intimacy. "Does Michel only worry about Mr. So-and-So or Mr. Such-and-such?" Now I'd be able to wonder if that were the case with the unfortunate foresight that he did and that what's despised isn't always despised for its just absence of value. As with my father, I hated having to defend him. If his own existence hadn't been enough, my help—conviction, admiration, love—would be a meager argument.

A sentence keeps running through my head: "Money was the least of his generosities." Money is one of the obvious links between author and publisher. But my father wanted to imbue the fact of being published by Minuit with such a symbolic charge that remuneration was secondary. He fought for each book he published and was happy to be able to pay a maximum of royalties for each, but that wasn't supposed to be the primary element in their relationship; and the writer wasn't supposed to count on it too soon. Perhaps what I'm maintaining is totally false, but that's the impression I had. Money came under the heading of power and tact.

One year when phone calls to other countries still seemed like the most extravagant thing in the world, I was going to be at rue de Vaugirard on Thierry's birthday while he himself was in Manila on a trip around the world that would end in Australia. Michel encouraged me to call from his place. After a moderate show of protest I accepted; and when the day arrived, I spoke to Thierry for a good three-quarters of any hour. I gave in easily without any scruples because I'd already decided to reimburse Michel by wiring the corresponding sum to his account, whose statements were often strewn over the large table in the apartment. My behavior came from the same idiotic pretension for refinement as the grand aunts of the narrator in *Remembrance of Things Past*, who thanked Swann in a way no one could understand. Hervé was often irked by what he saw as my father's stinginess and sometimes attributed the same to me, which led me to suspect that Michel thought so too. I was so convinced that a few weeks later, while lunching with Alain (the friend who hadn't shared acid with us because Michel hadn't either), I told him about what I'd done. "Oh," he answered, "I won't repeat that to Michel, of course." "Of course," I answered, despite the fact that I'd only spoken in hopes that he would. Suddenly aware that it wasn't going to happen, I felt even more disgraced by my attempt than by its failure.

Later, on Hervé's initiative, we both invited Michel to dinner. When the check came, Hervé took out a credit card and paid for everything. Michel thanked him as I sat there like an imbecile, and I privately reimbursed Hervé for half of it at our next dinner, where he responded in an offhand way to my reproach. I had the same excessive tact about money—in other words, the same lack of spontaneity—as I had for human relationships, as if it went on in some other world and called for perfect behavior. I was tangled in social signifiers and careful not to make too many. When my father died, his will gave me a bird's-eye view of how much his sense of economics was disconnected from any personal gain. A man assigned an audit to appraise the value of Les éditions de Minuit declared with a deadpan expression that the house was so well managed that it was a problem, because it would be impossible to cut the slightest cost if it became necessary. Immediately it occurred to me how much the way he was speaking would have gratified my father. He wanted the publishing house to have some reserves in case of a crisis, at which time he would have spent them to safeguard its independence. For him Les éditions de Minuit possessed considerable value, but not financially, because he would never have sold it, although his death transformed part of it into real money for me.

It was also only in reading *Jérôme Lindon* by Jean Echenoz that I learned that after Jean Rouaud's *Fields of Glory* (*Les Champs d'honneur*) received the prix Goncourt my father paid a bonus to "a certain number of authors of the house" because "in his eyes, such success wouldn't be complete if we weren't participating in it." When Jean Echenoz also won the Goncourt, my father gave out checks again. And I was even sorrier about not having known this while my father was alive, because I'd always been shocked in thinking that a publishing house was more financially devoted to its employees than to its authors; that in every company, be it tiny, average-sized or immense, there were more employees living on their salaries than authors on royalties.

I told Michel that I didn't like to talk about what I was writing because I feared that if I did I'd never end up writing it, because of a superstition originating with my family. Those rare times Minuit had announced in a book other books by the same author to appear, they hadn't. It turned out that this feeling was familiar to Michel. He told me he was annoyed with himself for not being able to repress a distressed expression coming over his face every time Daniel mentioned his own work to come because the announcement made Michel afraid that the book would never be written. But what distressed him later when he'd tell about it was his worry that Daniel might interpret his reaction as a kind of censure, some judgment about the ideas that had just been developed. And such excessive sensitivity on the part of Michel reminded me of my relationship to money because, independently of hard reality, it connected him to a lack of generosity. And for him, lacking generosity was like lacking intelligence. He would have had every reason to be surprised that this was happening to him.

In childhood, I unconsciously developed a gift that has never left me, that of spotting the étoile de Minuit—the logo of a star indicating that a book had been published by Les éditions de Minuit—on the spine of a book in a library and recognizing the typeface of the house when someone was reading next to me in the subway or on a train. That doesn't mean I lay claim to any responsibility for the house's success, but I had a link to that house that was expressed that way. And then, suddenly, I developed the same talent for the name *Foucault*, which today still pops out to my eyes in an article or on shelves full of books, as if I'd always been trained to notice it. Reading it revives something in me. Beckett himself would have seemed less deserving of his pedestal if he hadn't known this name and the texts that bore it. No matter how long he'd been close to James Joyce, he'd never met Michel. When it comes to that coup, Sam had been less talented than me.

9

I ran into my father one evening at a cocktail party at a publisher's, while he was talking with an incumbent minister. To keep from being interrupted, he'd pretended not to see me, until the minister noticed me and interrupted him, obviously to keep from showing any lack respect for a journalist who was also the son of such a publisher. I was always surprised that my father resembled the learned Cosinus,[1] in that way. He was full of exaggerated consideration for political men whom I thought couldn't hold a candle to him, and he himself must have been even more convinced of this. But obviously he saw an advantage for himself or for publishing and literature in behaving as he did, refusing to look at me, which also did nothing more than sanction a dominance over me in which the only use of having the upper hand became the right to such rudeness. Since the best thing you can teach your son is independence, the demonstration of it he gave was purely educational. I should have resisted, but like him I loathed conflicts because I'd obsessively take them all the way—to such an extent that I preferred not starting one. Indifference was often one of my strategies, as was refusing to be surprised. I made choices about the things for which it was worth going the whole mile.

---

1. Translator's note: Cosinus, a loopy fictional scientist from an 1893 comic strip.

My brother told me he asked him one day for some explanations about his relationship with my mother, and my father answered, "My life as part of a couple has nothing to do with you," to which my brother had retorted, "Except for the fact that your couple is my family." Never would I have been able to ask such a question. My father and mother?—that didn't have anything to do with me. I didn't need to know a thing about it. When I spent some time at a friend's place who was crazy about young guys to the extent that he paraded them in his home in front of his son, who ended up being unsettled by it, my friend, who was close to becoming exasperated, complained to me one day, "Why's he getting involved? It feels like he wants to dictate my personal life." If I'd interrupted my father at the cocktail party to greet him, what would have annoyed him would have obviously also been the fact I was undermining his personal life, an intrusion that nothing justified when the ministerial function of the man he was talking to made it abundantly clear that this was a question of serious business. Once Sam had recounted that on one occasion Joyce had said to him in a tone meant to keep him at a distance something like, "Nothing is more important than family," and all of us had resented the author of *Ulysses* when we learned about it. My father was a barefaced competitor who had no intention of writing better books than Joyce but was determined to outdo him by not explicitly awarding any exaggerated importance to the same family that he'd spend the last years of his life trying to unite—after it was too late.

Even so, I had thought that my father was putting too much into that episode with the minister, especially since a few years before, Michel had met with the same man while he was already serving in that capacity and told me about it with a wide smile, saying, "He deserved being treated as an idiot already, just not yet at the Ministry."

One day a few years earlier, the minister Michel found so stupid invited me and two or three other journalists on a brief trip to Germany where he was supposed to give a speech, returning that same afternoon. My father was happy for me about that social privilege, the fact that I was going to be part of the minister's team; whereas I'd had fun acting like a naughty smart aleck by sneaking into the toilets of the French government's little military plane on which some conscripts were substituting for stewardesses so I could snort a few lines of heroin. When I got back, however, Michel dampened any thought of rebellious pride by claiming I should never have made the trip (a type of thing I never did again): "A journalist, yes. A writer, no." I had just published my first novel, but I hadn't yet really grasped what a writer was. Although this text had created a conflict with my father, and the second was going to do the same, for the time being I was withdrawing from the old rapport that had bound my father and me. The relationship was displaced, allowing my father's domination to grow exponentially, because there was now no one left (well, almost no one) on my side to stand up to it. No more fighting was possible because he'd set out to conquer a territory I was abandoning for another that was more to my taste and where I was becoming inaccessible—jinxing any added happiness we could have derived from our bonds.

My father's ambition had always been to add Michel to the list of his authors, and he figured my friendship with him might make it easier. I would have been happy if it could have. Michel had met him at the publisher's after seeing and very much liking my brother's film. My father had snagged a meeting from it where he was hoping to convince Michel to give him a book, an affair Michel didn't dwell on with me. Instead he told me that my father had developed a theory based on Hervé's work and my brother's. And Michel added that this viewpoint had seemed completely false to him, but he expressed this indifferently, almost regrettably, being more sensitive to my father's taste than to his explanations. Becoming a writer of literature was distancing me from my father and bringing me closer to Michel. I thought my father had had misgivings about my work because its author was his son, in other words, for a bad reason. In his own way, Michel made me understand that it was a good one, or at least an allowable one for the time being, even if it wasn't being expressed. In fact, all I'd had to do was to submit my first manuscript to another publisher right away so that nothing would have come up. But my father had taught me to think of books—some of them—highly, and I was calling for his literary judgment. When the media or any kind of snobbism granted one of the novels or social science books he published unexpected raves, he claimed it was a misunderstanding, as if the purity of literature or sociology or philosophy were being betrayed by commercial success, which he nonetheless appreciated for its correct value. It was as if only bad reasons expropriated the stainless elitism from such works, and the only good reasons for appreciating them were his, just as I thought they were mine.

And yet the whole subject of my first novel is a father prostituting his children, while they submit to it extremely graciously, since it's a question of sex, which is appealing on many occasions, as if they were being told to mend his socks, an activity full of fun in any context. My father had no scruples about using me— my almost inexistent resistance didn't stop him—so without my realizing it in my alarmingly dumbfounded state, my novel challenged a system of functioning that far exceeded my genital apparatus' and aspired to no true genitality. In my family imagery, a father served his son in concrete terms, which mine had done by giving me his name, which I was the first to value in the most respectable way possible. He discreetly intervened on my behalf in a way that was refined and—I couldn't help thinking next—placed a card in his hand in case of tension, a potential weapon of dissuasion looming up unexpectedly. When reciprocity appeared to me, it seemed unequal, like trickery. The way he made use of me affected my daily life and my strategy for confronting the world, ways of thinking I had believed were personal. Something inside him, even including his way of noticing that I was taking after him, persisted in tainting his own generosity, whereas circumstances made Michel's blazingly evident. Returning years after to the pseudonym under which my first novel had appeared and with which he also wanted me to sign the next, I saw it: my father had given me his name and then taken it back, surprised that each of his wishes weren't followed and that name blessed more easily. Michel had offered me one I regretted not having been faithful to from book to book. My father wanted it so insistently and for such a bad reason that it had turned me away from it—he wanted it for him and the family. I would have had to want it for myself.

If Michel had seen me while he was talking to the minister in front of whom my father had snubbed me, I was persuaded he would have enjoyed snubbing the minister instead by rushing over to me, more amused by inflicting rudeness on the Big Wheel than on the little cog. To be honest, I was completely certain that the esteem my father showed this minister was feigned, dependent on the politician's consent to his own arguments, diagnoses and remedies, on his usefulness. He didn't admire the man but the function, or rather, didn't admire it but was making do with it. He was the first to place writers, and especially those he published, miles above men of politics and in some way thought of himself as the intermediary or spokesperson for his authors in this shady world, a role that allowed him to exercise the power for which he served as agent while keeping his writers from being sullied. For his part, Michel, who wasn't a novelist, didn't need anyone to inform the person currently in power what he thought of him. From my perspective, when journalism made me rub shoulders with politicians, I showed them respect without anything at stake, without truth and out of pure convenience. Finding myself having to exchange a few words with this famous minister, since he was tanned, I timidly found nothing better to say than, "You're looking good." I'd barely finished that sentence before I regretted it and immediately felt wretched because of the remark's other, undesired meaning. Unexpectedly he answered, "But you know, I work a lot," and that was the extent of my relations with that world. On this point I was accepting being the son of my father 100%: my world was books, and often also their authors.

The first long article I did for *Le Nouvel Observateur* entailed spending a week in Hyères, where there was a film festival characterized as avant-garde or "alternative." I was excited by such novelty and terrorized at having to confront so many unknown people. I had just met Michel, Gérard and Hervé and still didn't feel nearly up to snuff to face human relations. As chance would have it, among the jury of the festival were both Alain Robbe-Grillet and Marguerite Duras, permitting me to feel as if I were on familiar terrain. I wasn't conscious of being special, which reduced my shyness in this place where such a distinction would have led to the opposite by creating it. Robbe-Grillet loved making fun of the world, and I was an easy target. This suited me because in it I saw a kind of fraternity, a word he had used in one of his dedications. I sensed that he liked me a lot even so. There is often respect in humor, which by nature invites you to share in it. When Valéry Giscard d'Estaing, the president of the Republic, had claimed on Bernard Pivot's TV show that he certainly would have liked being Flaubert or Maupassant, I'd made the banal remark if he had been Flaubert, it would have been surprising to see him write both *Madame Bovary* and *Démocratie française*, a book by the president that was being published at the time. Alain had answered, "But if he'd been Flaubert, maybe he wouldn't have written *Madame Bovary*," and I took in my share of his irony, as I already wanted to be a writer without yet having anything that proved it. In Hyères, Alain introduced me to various people by saying that this was the first time I'd left my room, having spent my entire life reading until that very moment. At this point I didn't know what made that obvious but it was one of my characteristics. Michel as well laughed when he mentioned an author to me and I said I hadn't read him, as if unearthing such a rare bird had been a real feat. I rarely thought much of myself, but I was noticing that my appetite for literary binging—for me merely a sort of hedonism I would never have thought to boast about—provoked a certain respect. However, I was just as snobbish about reading as I was about famous people and kept quiet about what I had done and whom I knew. I hit it off with a heap of people at the festival during my week in Hyères, which was pure joy. I was an escapee.

After Hervé died, a biography of him appeared. In it I fell upon a passage in which the author was interviewing my father about his opinion of Hervé in which my father answered, "I've always had respect for Mathieu's friends." When I discovered that sentence, I first found it ridiculous. It discredited the book, given that it was the only remark the author had believed fitting to put into my father's mouth on the subject, as if this were all he had to say about Hervé, whose seven books he had published over the years. But Hervé was dead and wasn't reading the text. They'd never reconciled, not to mention that my father hadn't the same respect for biographies that he felt for literary works (and I'd been contaminated by that opinion). Perhaps these words were intended for me. In any case it was to my interest to think so because it mattered to me. Just as my first homosexual adventures had been encouraged by the respect Valérie had for her lovers, who became mine, warranting my choices, so was it simpler when my father ratified my choice of friends.

Hervé had come to Les éditions de Minuit through me, via the review I edited, and the first time Hervé entrusted me with a book-length manuscript, my father made sure to refuse it to avoid relying on me, eventually accepting *Ghost Image* (*L'Image fantôme*) when it had come to him by another path. However, a few months before—obviously so I'd transmit it myself—he'd reported to me that Sam had read a text by Hervé in the review that he found remarkable ("La Piqûre d'amour"[2]). For my father there was no greater compliment than one from Samuel Beckett, and I myself could share it at the same time in my role as publisher of the text and friend of the author. He was dishing out some respect to me.

Well after my father's death, one of his favorite authors used the same word while telling me he'd signed his first contract without reading it because he thought my father would have had less respect for him if he'd acted differently. It was a custom in the profession for the first contract to specify five books from the author. It was the same kind of contract my father had had Hervé sign, but since his first texts all came from different genres (essay, novel, autobiographical account, book of photos), all requiring a specific contract, Hervé had ended up owing such a ridiculous number of books when he'd become angry with my father that my father had been able to do nothing but free him from them. When my second novel continued to cause problems and I decided to have my work published elsewhere, which in the long run proved wise as it also brokered the revival of a bond between us, my father, whom I apparently no longer disturbed, asked me for my next book as a peaceful way for me to finish off that stage of our relationship. However, even I preferred the return of my contract to save myself from the possibility of his using it as

2. Translator's note: Literally, "The Sting of Love" or "The Shot [Injection] of Love."

blackmail in the future. As it had for Hervé, my father's distrust caused suspicion. When the author spoke to me about the way he'd signed his contract, I didn't know if it had created more respect in my father's eyes than his novel itself had been worth, but I was certain my father would have made him pay if he'd shilly-shallied, would have demonstrated his monetary implacability if the writer had shown an interest in such issues considered unwholesome, almost anti-literary.

For me, everything that had to do with Hervé also had to do with Michel, who'd been the sponsor of our relationship from its first day. And naturally my father had respect not only for Michel but also for the bond that I was forging with him that my father in no way shared. Similarly, my father must have felt up to the fact of my remaining friends with Hervé, to which he contributed by his reserve after they had become angry at each other. I had constructed my hole where I could live my life according to my affections without betraying anyone. My father had no expectation that I'd fall out with Michel if he ever did, as had happened when he'd become angry with his parents during my adolescence and I hadn't seen them during those years—out on my own wish, of course, with all my independence of mind. On the contrary, he would have preferred becoming close with Michel since I was, or, in any case, becoming his publisher, through a process that would have been the opposite of the usual one. He would have preferred it, and he was expert at applying pressure, but he never pressured me for that. "He exaggerates," Michel had ended up saying once, when I was updating him hour by hour on my editorial-familial disputes regarding the manuscript of my two first novels. Exaggeration was actually the price my father often paid for his passion, and he perpetually had a goal, a solution, in mind. Michel never exaggerated for a second during all those years, never with a word—out of nobility and intelligence, respect and a sharp awareness of power struggles.

THESE YEARS

One day when we were talking about Napoleon and the carnage he caused, Michel got a kick out of my lack of historical sense when I mentioned that all those people would be dead by now anyway. Perhaps Michel and my father wouldn't have needed AIDS or cancer to be just as deceased as they are today. Those times are dead even if others who will be are still young.

I'd spoken about Napoleon's soldiers that way because I saw only one position to pretend for showing solidarity with these victims. Using words to signal obvious good sentiment is no sign of commitment to anything. Solidarity is something else. It reminds me of Bernardo's rejoinder after Hervé died seven-and-a-half years after Michel, when we were discussing AIDS victims and he said I was one. To me this seemed obscene. AIDS victims were the ones who'd been sick, died, not those who loved them. I would have usurped compassion by claiming such a thing, and you had to be Napoleon to merit being a usurper. My education had convinced me that everything was due to my father, and only my belief and affection persuaded me that it was all due to Michel.

The same for being a writer. I had always deeply identified with it, and it was enough for me to know it without claiming it to convince others before I'd even written. Being able to practice it is the first thing I require from writing. Once Michel told me that, unlike me, Hervé would die if he couldn't write; and he wasn't implying anything sacred or conclusive by that remark. He himself believed he could have done something else in life. Later, Hervé declaring he'd go nuts or kill someone if he didn't write struck me. I myself might have gone nuts—unless I was already—but I'd never say it. I'm nuts when I write.

***

I receive a very thick, unknown book at the newspaper. Its structure, a series of brief texts or fables of doubtful morality, as well as the title and opening lines, *The Pleasantries of the Incredible Mulla Nasrudin* (*Sublimes paroles et idioties de Nasr Eddin Hodja*),[1] attract me to such a degree that I become immersed in it with pleasure that comes close to fascination. It's a collection of very ancient anecdotes around a legendary figure of the Muslim world that remind me of Jewish tales. I would have loaned it to my father if that were still possible, because I'm confident the book would amuse him. Among the hundreds of texts in the volume, my favorite is called "L'essence de mon enseignement."[2] A crafty, dishonest and appealing moron named Mulla Nasrudin is teaching some young students when the father of one of them arrives to give him a plate of baklava. A moment later, the master is called outside. Fearing they'll be eaten in his absence, he warns the children that the sweets are poisoned. Nevertheless the cakes are devoured the moment he

---

1. Translator's note: The French title is, literally, *Nasr Eddin's Magnificent Words and Stupidities*. The author is Indries Shah, born in India to a family descended from Afghan nobles. The book is redolent with Sufi mysticism, based on lectures Shah gave at the University of Geneva. He considered these tales pedagogical, part of an entire course of study.
2. Translator's note: Literally, "The Essence of My Teaching."

has left the room. On Mulla Nasrudin's return, he's greeted with a sorry spectacle: not the smallest piece of baklava remains, his porcelain inkwell is in a thousand pieces and the children are doubled up in pain. He takes them to task until they offer an explanation. "Oh, master!" one of them succeeds in saying while groaning in pain, "don't speak harshly. We'd been so ashamed of breaking your inkwell that we all committed suicide by eating the poison cakes."

"Ah! Get back on your feet, dear children. Congratulations for having so well understood the essence of my teaching."

At the end of 2004, I meet Corentin, and everything goes wonderfully in the bar and back at my place. We don't sleep for a second—something that hasn't happened to me for years. We make love, talk. For some reason we happen to mention psychoanalysis. I tell him I'm not familiar with it and that the only thing I really know about it is that a friend of mine had good reasons to claim you should never fall in love with a boy who is in analysis. "I'm in analysis," he answers with a smile. And I'm smiling, too, kissing him because, obviously, it has no importance. It's just a rule for living that hasn't been tested by circumstances. The friend whod tole me to beware of boys in psychoanalysis was Michel, although there's not the slightest reason to compare him to Mulla Nasrudin when it comes to anything at all. I feel faithful to his teaching, which he never presented as such and did not respect. He as well was smiling.

Before knowing Michel, I'd tried psychoanalysis on one occasion, but I hadn't been wild enough about the guy to go back. I told Michel about it, adding that the money it cost had played a discouraging role. Michel found that an excellent motive for giving up. I answered that it had taken courage to try it, but I was also having trouble convincing myself that it was courageous to give it up so lickety-split. In fact, all of the shrinks I next encountered dissuaded me from going into it with the pretext that I didn't need it, and every time I hated myself for how talented I was at duping each of them. However, while my father was still alive—in view of my state of mind— I just couldn't do other than see a psychoanalyst—someone I liked and whom Bernardo had recommended. She, too, insisted a cure wasn't necessary but promised to be available whenever I needed her. A week after my second session, I saw an article in *Le Monde* announcing her death. I took it as a premonition, but not a minor or ambiguous one, not a totally personal interpretation, as they can be, but a momentous foreboding, a kick from a corpse that mixed superstition, science and magic. *Basta*, for psychoanalysis and me.

Even so, I'm certain she would have had a word to say about the epidemic of deaths occurring around me during a certain period, although no "friend's death" had the celebrity import of a first-rate "father's death." There was a time when my sadness took on the aspect of a curse. As if I were a sinister King Midas, all those I became close to died. I felt that, despite myself, I was gifted with some malevolent power and was surviving in the midst of such carnage only at that price. This feeling peaked when my grandfather died, despite the fact that his passing was the least shocking. He was old and ended up dying from his cancer. But his death occurred a few weeks after Hervé's, which was expected and in truth desired, although that feature removed none of its horrible nature. I was consumed with woe at the perspective of having to go to the cemetery every month for someone close to me. It wasn't what I was expecting of life. Moreover, I had just met Rachid. I was already crazy about him and would have wanted him to go with me to the funeral. That wasn't a possibility for various reasons: he'd gone back to Morocco—reason enough—but he was also male, North African and fifteen years younger than me. Any of my cousins could have gone with his girlfriend but not me with him, and that irritated me even though it wasn't even a possibility and was only happening in my head. I imagined everybody looking at me strangely, not to mention what Rachid would have felt about being there. Also, without explaining his personal feelings, my father would just have been unhappy about his son having made a bad impression, would have reproached me like an impartial judge for not having taken into account such a foreseeable reaction.

A few years after Michel's death, I thought that a moment would come when the time gone by would exceed the number of years I had known him, and that thought resurfaced regularly. When Hervé died, that day had already arrived. And another day came, marking a longer time since Hervé had died than the period during which we'd been close. With my father, of course, that's far from happening (unless I almost reach my hundreds). The six years spent with Michel represent a more and more minute percentage of my existence, which nevertheless ceaselessly increases in the most sincere part of my imagination. Comparing years to years is adding up apples and oranges and has nothing to do with the mathematics of existence. But the figures fascinate me.

That first night, as I get to know Corentin, he informs me he's studying at the Grande École for the training of teachers, in the department of philosophy. I ask him about the contemporary philosophers—contemporary for me, since Michel has been dead for more than twenty years—and he answers that he's not very familiar with them, except for Foucault whose reading did him a world of good. The boy seems better and better to me. I'm surprised by his youth. I ask his age, and when he answers, the exact date of his birth. It turns out that he was born after the death of Michel. I quickly calculate that the difference of age between us is the same as it was between Michel and me.

When Michel was alive and my affection for him was its most intense, I'd hoped there'd be someone my age to love me as much and be as devoted to me when I became his age. But that fantasy was projected into such a faraway future that I never expected it would become reality. It was mostly a way to revel in my relationship with Michel and bask in my position—sentimental masturbation. As it turns out, when I become aware of the precise difference in age between Corentin and me, it actually doesn't call to mind Michel and me at all. There would be too much pretension and too little resemblance in my identifying with Michel, even only on this point. To me it seems more like coincidence, an anecdote that is all the less meaningful from the fact that I have no idea of the future of my connection with Corentin, whom I'm only spending one memorable night with, despite my immediate impression that it's pointing to something more. But I'm unreservedly convinced that our difference in age produces no harmful effect and that there's nothing to fear. I'm confident about such a relationship because I know it can work. It's one of lessons that I kept from Michel, from Michel and me, actually; and it even became so natural to me that I need the distance of writing to become aware I could have thought otherwise.

A year after our encounter, Corentin and I go abroad for a week of vacation. The day after our arrival, I realize I must have got up to piss during the night because I regain consciousness lying on the bathroom floor. Since adolescence, I've had low blood pressure that has caused me to black out on quite a few occasions, so I unworriedly go back to bed. After a few minutes, I'm still not feeling very well. As soon as Corentin opens his eyes, I tell him what just happened and ask him if we can go quickly to the breakfast they must have started serving that should restore some of my strength. But during breakfast I still feel ill. Corentin takes me back to the room, and the hotel doctor arrives rapidly. When he learns my name, he asks if I'm from the actor's family rather than my father's. Used as I am to eluding that kind of question, I clearly tell him that he's talking about my first cousin. I must be worried if I'm using that ploy to assure I'll get the best care. In spite of the fact that my blood pressure is actually normal now, I pass out again, accompanied by some spectacular convulsions—I'll later learn. The doctor has me immediately transferred to a hospital. The ride is horrible, and I don't realize that I'm losing consciousness again and again. Corentin will tell me that I became literally incommunicable, icy cold and incommunicable. The only relief I feel during a moment of consciousness is that I've changed a part of my will since I met Corentin. I give him the code for my cell phone so that he can call Rachid and Gérard in case. Later he'll tell me about the state of anxiety he was in; but for the moment, I don't sense any coming from him, and his presence only serves to calm me—it's the polar opposite of what happened to Michel and me during that acid trip.

At the hospital it turns out that my survival has been something of a miracle during the last twenty-four hours, but it still depends on a very simple operation, which goes perfectly. By the following morning I'm out of my predicament. When I get back to my room after a day in recovery, I call Rachid. After I met him, when he was living in Morocco, I'd phoned him every day. At the beginning, I was afraid of putting pressure on him by behaving this way; but once he told me how much it would matter to him if my daily phone calls to Marrakech ended. I'd only missed calling him the day before. There had been no reason to worry him by announcing my operation since after it I would need hours before I achieved a state in which I could offer any news. So I pour out my heart all at once, telling him I'd almost died and that now I'm back hale and hearty. I'm still a bit groggy, but relieved. He, meanwhile, has been sped through the states I experienced; and at the end of my rushed account, I realize he's still feeling shattered. Certainly his mother had died, but without his ever having known her. This is a drama of another order. He still doesn't know that even the people you love the most and take the greatest care of can die. You only learn that as you go along.

A male nurse goes with me as I leave the recovery room. In front of the other nurses, he gives me a kind of ice compartment for medicines, with three little drawers marked morning, noon and evening repeated ten times. I thank him, whereas the others laugh. The surgeon had told me I wouldn't need any treatment after the operation. In my mindless state, the only thing I wonder next is whether this nurse, who seems like a smug airhead, is being hostile, whether having Corentin along—seeing he's of the same sex, or of a different age, or both—has been making me seem unlikeable and that I'm undergoing a hazing. That thought only enters my mind—in the opposite sense—after a female friend who was miraculously also there on vacation tells me the doctor asked her before the operation if Corentin was my son. "No," she answered. "Is it his boyfriend?" he then asked. "Yes," she answered. "He seems to love him very much. That's good," the doctor said. The conversation and its kindly indiscretion touch me. Corentin also tells me that he was waiting in the hallway during the operation and that it had barely ended when the doctor came to tell him that everything had gone well, in a manner not at all the kind you'd use with a son. The nurse is a lesser evil. I'm glad this adventure happened to me out of the country, far from all bureaucracy. I think of Michel, because everything that has to do with death makes me think of him; of my father, because I always remember what Proust said in correspondence after the death of his mother: his only small consolation was that it kept his mother from surviving him. I finish this trip feeling euphoric because it has made my intimacy with Corentin stronger than even the most intense acid trip could do. It's not like surviving an epidemic, only about my own death.

There are no more long trips until a recent one to Egypt with Corentin. When we arrive at the hotel the first evening, the receptionist seems surprised and speaks a few words in Arabic into the telephone. We connect this to the fact that a minute after we've reached the room, two men with a bed for one person suddenly appear and install it at a distance from the large one, which had been the only bed. We aren't amused. Such a thing never happened with Rachid. Is it because he's about fifteen years older than Corentin, or simply because Egypt is not Morocco? It's disconcerting. I'm in no mood for activism, so I put up with it and give the two men the expected tip, although in my eyes they're far from deserving it. After all, we don't need to make more of a scene than not sleeping in the small bed. The next afternoon, the telephone rings when we're alone in the room and whoever it is hangs up when I answer, pandering to our paranoia, as if any method were good enough to keep us from having sex. I'm thinking that if Corentin and I had the same last name, if it were possible to suspect I was his father, the personnel of the hotel would be less particular. Any child at all is a visa for the social world; paternity rules out bad mores.

Who'd think that I'd suddenly ask myself such a question? What kind of father am I, who have no child? It's as if I at times give way to convention, that a relationship between two beings separated by loads of years necessarily brings fatherhood into play, despite the fact that its sexual nature would then imply incest at the least. Such a thing had never crossed my mind for a second when Michel was alive. I loved him as Michel, not at all as a father. I never felt the slightest jealousy toward him nor the slightest bitterness, the slightest exasperation, which nobody is entitled to expect from the best son or lover.

On Google I discover that a line from *Endgame*, "Nothing is funnier than unhappiness…" is now the subject of a dissertation. When I was small, in our home it became a blithe aphorism whose wit my brother and I would savor when the Becketts came to dinner. We'd noticed that there was always a moment in the conversation when the mood was no longer one of gaiety and Suzanne and Sam would mention various catastrophes that inevitably occurred—for example, the death of the actor in London who'd created a particular Beckett role, or of a theater director who'd been the first to produce a certain play in New York or Berlin. Our parents showed solidarity with tearful expressions, which were de rigueur. My brother and I, thrilled and proud to see things turning out just as we'd expected, were on the verge of bursting out laughing, which we knew was bad taste, although it always threatened to happen to me as an adult at the cemetery.

Ever since I've known Rachid, as soon as I announce the death of a member of my group who isn't very close, he smiles. This surprised me the first time, but even then it didn't shock me. There's no ill will in his smile, nothing satirical. He's only noticing an inadequacy when comparing the drama of death to the pain it's worth to me, bearable after all is said and done; just as he might raise an eyebrow in hearing the words, "I love you" spoken offhandedly or strategically. Sincerity is so much a feature of relationships for him that he sees every disparity as an infraction.

Since I have known him, the thing I've feared most has been the death of his father. I was afraid of the same thing when it came to Hassan II[3] and its consequences for Rachid in Morocco, and I was wrong. But Rachid's father is a fantastic person, wonderful and magical. I've never met him, only heard him

3. Translator's note: the king of Morroco (1929–1999).

mentioned in conversation with Rachid or encountered him in his books. A few years ago, Rachid told me, "You're like my father: you want only my good," and that moved me. The comparison was a limited one; both of us know the point at which our bond doesn't resemble that of father and son. But there's nothing ambivalent in his feelings for his father. All baseness or bitterness seems foreign to their relationship. Rachid knew how to depict such a character, and not only to my eyes. In *Ce qui reste*,[4] there's a scene that had already staggered me when he'd told it in person. "You've just called me with the words, 'Rachid, my son, come eat.' I love when you say 'my son.' Immediately I feel a breath of freedom flowing from me. It's crazy, because I know I'll make you uncomfortable by telling you that not so long ago a reader of around twenty-five stopped me at a shopping mall in Paris, because he recognized me, and said, 'Aren't you Rachid O.? Is your father doing o.k.? That's all I wanted to know, so, thanks.' I stopped and hid under an escalator to cry without being seen because something warm streamed through me, something I wasn't expecting at all." Father and son brought tears to my own eyes with that exchange. I so wish someone could have asked me the same question in the same circumstances, by my having created so much affection for a human being through literature. It must be pure joy to have given birth to your own father.

A few weeks ago, although I don't know what his family knows about me, Rachid repeated what his father had said about me, without specifying what he himself said that provoked it, and its benevolence moved me because I could still deduce it from the wording of his father's answer: "He's older than you. You'll need to be there when he needs you." It's a blessing that includes me.

───────────

4. Translator's note: In English, literally, *What Remains*.

However, Rachid's father is no longer doing well at all. He has suddenly died. Rachid calls me to tell me that he's going back for the funeral and arrives in Morocco just in time to see his father still alive, but in what a state. His grief is painful to hear. I'm ashamed at my feeling of helplessness. He isn't calling to share his suffering but so I'll try to console him an iota. That doesn't change the fact that his father is dead, and I have nothing to say because I feel committed to honesty, crushed by solidarity, closeness, and our love is such a good conductor of grief, transmitting it at the speed of electricity. My imagination is of no use to me at all. Yes, the people you love die and don't come back to life. Reality is terrifying. You always end up lacking enough humor to taste the unjust mirth of misfortune.

When he gets back to Paris and I speak with him in person, using the phrase "your father's death," he's still smiling in his sadness. Because as much as I love Rachid and loved my father, this is the death of his own father. Whatever my suffering may be, his is inaccessible to me. I'm helpless. A fear has linked me to Rachid from the start, a fear that is love. It's like that for my father and Michel, and also for Corentin and Gérard: dread—terror—about not being able to prevent misfortune from striking the loved one. As if I weren't getting an advantage by not being the father of those I love, being nothing, physiologically speaking, in their existence. It's as if, despite myself, I was becoming part of the bad side of fatherhood, a responsibility that takes aim, chokes and distorts. I need the other's help to find a way out.

It turns out that Corentin isn't in too great a shape either these days—he's a young man. He doesn't know how to organize his life, what to do with it. He's afraid his studies serve only to fritter away the present for him. The guy who's subletting him a room is misbehaving, and he has to move in a rush. His intelligence doesn't always make life easier for him. He can't yet imagine what kind of work will allow him to make a living without weighing on him terribly. He feels as if nothing sticks to him, everything escapes. And no matter to what length I go to make him change his state of mind, I'm still baffled when I have to confront the stubborn fact that he gets discouraged at times and that the helplessness and annoyance it provokes in me can only drive it in more. "It's not a big deal to be depressed," he says to me one evening with a smile that infects me. On that day everything is simpler. Listening to him, letting him speak without pressure is already something, just as my being there with those feelings was certainly no small matter for Michel. Whether young or old, when two people are separated by a significant difference in age, I'm always the one being taught. I'm the hero of a perpetual coming-of-age novel, permanently being reeducated.

I see Rachid and Corentin's potent clear-sightedness as a generational link because it's the norm for younger people to understand that such behavior isn't justified by a moral doctrine but by the obsessions and characteristics of those older than them with which they feel themselves obliged (or not) to make do, protecting their elders like I've felt I was doing a hundred times. That isn't how I was with Michel. I wish he'd known Rachid and Corentin, too, so he could help them, better than I can. Obviously it isn't enough to have grown older to be like him; you'd need to be him. And yet, I feel as if Rachid and Corentin, not to mention myself, are directly in line with the education you can draw from *The Use of Pleasure* and *The Care of the Self*—the two books that appeared a few days before Michel died and on which he had worked so much—through Corentin reading them and Rachid not needing to. I love the way each listens to me when I succeed at talking about Michel. I would have wanted to be able to duplicate the education Michel gave me, and I was dismayed to discover it was beyond my powers. Still, part of that education reoccurred on its own, automatically, in tune with the idea Michel often expressed about psychoanalysis, in which the quality of the analyst is secondary to the process itself. Haven't both Michel and my father transmitted a way of loving to me? Each of them. There's a way to love and a way to be loved.

There are times when people mention their relationship with my father to me in a way they think is flattering, whereas according to my analysis of the account it's hardly any reason to brag. It makes me uncomfortable, but I don't intervene; it's not up to me to clear up misunderstandings that my father willingly allowed to foster, or to correct his strategy, even at this post-mortem stage. One day someone who'd met Michel less than three times claimed having spoken with him about my father and me, figuring it was flattering to repeat such information. It struck me as crude, but I didn't say a thing, either; speaking of which, I'm perfectly aware that nobody but me is asking me to be faithful to Michel, whereas not dishonoring my father's name is an affair belonging to the public sector. When I was ten, twenty, forty-five or fifty-five I was always his son, where-as Michel could never have been the friend he was for a kid of eight. But that's fatherhood: having ever loved a child means having had him over a barrel.

"What would be the worth of struggling for knowledge if that only allowed it to a certain degree, without taking those who know beyond their own identity in some way, to the extent that this is possible? There are moments in life when the question of knowing whether you can think differently than you do and perceive differently than you see is indispensable in order to keep on looking and keep on reflecting." Michel wrote this in the introduction to *The Use of Pleasure*, which he was working on during our relationship. And long before knowing him I remember how much I'd been struck by words in the introduction to *The Order of Things* (*Les Mots et les Choses*) in which he describes his growing laughter while reading the description of a system of classification in a text by Jorge Luis Borges: "the stark impossibility of thinking *that*." Thinking differently was, in addition to those moments spent with us, also what he hoped to find in acid. As incompetent at philosophy as Hervé and I were, having indulged in no formal study of the subject, we were still more likely to be of help—to reveal new avenues of thought just by chance or out of ignorance or imagination—compared with those whose education was more like his and only lacked intelligence and courage. That's also why it seemed obvious to me that Rachid and his books would have pleased Michel a great deal, and I was happy to see that Daniel shared that certainty. To live is to live differently.

Michel's legacy is that possibility of creating unlikely relationships and maintaining them all at the same time, without such simultaneity being a problem. On the one hand, nothing moved me as much as fidelity; on the other, this seemed like a wanton case of sloth. Michel was amused that the *mil e tre*[5] partners that made Don Juan so monstrous would be accomplished in three years by any fag who goes out every night. Sometimes I find the requirement of sexual fidelity to be a disgrace.

***

Because a problem with rights prohibited showing most of Charlie Chaplin's feature films during my childhood, I wasn't able to see them until I became a teenager. In one of the first to be rereleased, I remember Charlie returning home and

---

5. Translator's note: meaning "one thousand three," from Leporello's aria in Mozart's *Don Giovanni*.

opening the door, which makes a plank fall on his head. This scene happens three, five times, because Charlie is always thinking of something else as he pushes open that door, until the moment comes when he's paying attention, which doesn't change a thing. No matter how cautiously he opens his door, the plank still falls on his head. I loved that gag. Since the film had been unable to be seen for years, the next day *Le Journal du dimanche* asked some young members of the audience their reactions, and one of them said he'd liked the film except for the slapstick with the plank, which he thought was repetitive. Good teenager that I was, I'd felt flattered about having such original taste.

Later, I drew a kind of metaphor from that scene. For me, the essence of the gag depends on the importance of Charlie's distraction for the viewer, the way he keeps forgetting about the danger of the plank. However, when he opens the door little by little, precisely because he's remembering the danger, the plank still bops him on the mug, because its falling doesn't depend on the attention Charlie gives it but on the angle of the door as it opens. When the door goes beyond the allowed angle only by a half degree, the plank comes tumbling down, whether Charlie is worried about it or not. When I was young, I found I was intelligent. Then I realized that I was stupid, as well, but I thought that such an observation was a sign of intelligence. Finally, I couldn't go any further than the discovery that when I was stupid, that's just what I was; knowing it didn't change anything.

I'm a necrophile: I keep loving the dead. Like a teenager who can't resist masturbating, I can't help it. Necrophilia isn't a sexual vice but an affectionate affection. This book has been my way of taking my own loves captive. When I was very young, I was lucky enough for the death of those I loved to remain in the beyond—of my existence. Then I had to face the fact that Michel's death was a plank of unknown scale that devastated my head and entire body. I managed to adapt to it. Death also isn't devoid of sweetness as the years pass. But each of us knows that it can reemerge in all its harshness at the hazard of a memory or an association. The last time I stop by rue de Vaugirard before going out to dinner with Daniel, an unpleasant noise never stops during that entire visit. When I finally ask him about it, he explains that the elevator has been renovated, causing a defect that the managing agent is in no hurry to repair. A ridiculous sadness floods me at the thought that the old Mahler corner is dead for a thousand reasons, and now for this one as well.

I would have liked to write this book with the idea in mind of Michel and my father reading it with emotion, if its basis hadn't been the stark impossibility of their doing such a thing with any feeling at all—it's unthinkable. It brings to my mind the sinister Carambar[6] joke about the master of an adored dog now dead, who faced with the bones of its corpse, regrets that the dog can't even enjoy them: at one moment or another, this is every love story.

6. Translator's note: Carambar is a brand of candies in France that contain corny jokes written on the inside of their wrappers.

ABOUT THE AUTHOR

Mathieu Lindon, born in 1955, is a French writer and a journalist at *Libération*. He won the Prix Médecis in 2011 for the publication of *Ce qu'aimer veut dire* (*Learning What Love Means*).